Wisdom of the Celtic Saints

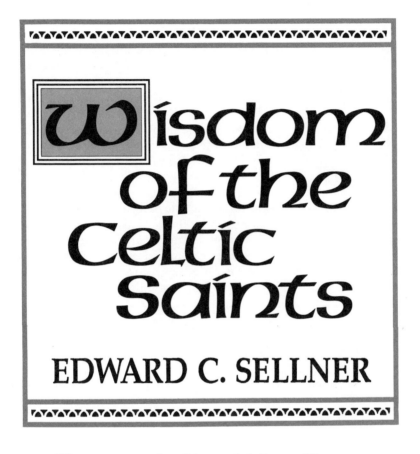

Wisdom of the Celtic Saints

EDWARD C. SELLNER

Illustrations by Susan McLean-Keeney

AVE MARIA PRESS Notre Dame, Indiana 46556

Edward Sellner is associate professor of pastoral theology and spirituality at the College of St. Catherine in St. Paul, Minnesota, where he is also director of the masters program in theology. Sellner, who holds a doctorate in theology from the University of Notre Dame, is the author of numerous journal articles. His books include *Mentoring: The Ministry of Spiritual Kinship* (Ave Maria Press) and *Soul-Making: The Telling of a Spiritual Journey* (Twenty-Third Publications).

Artist **Susan McLean-Keeney** is a graduate of the Fine Arts program of the University of Minnesota where she also earned a master's degree in art history. As a Fulbright Exchange Teacher in and a frequent traveller to the British Isles, she has visited and studied many of the celtic holy sites which she illustrates. McLean-Keeney is an art instructor at Coon Rapids High School and has taught for Inver Hills Community College, both in Minnesota.

© 1993 by Ave Maria Press, Notre Dame, IN 46556

International Standard Book Number: 0-87793-492-4

Library of Congress Catalog Card Number: 92-74778

Cover and text design by Elizabeth J. French

Printed and bound in the United States of America.

For my students, past and present,
and
for Thomas Merton, my guide

In every generation wisdom lives in holy souls
and makes them friends of God.
(Wisdom 7:27)

Friendship is nothing else but wisdom.
(Aelred of Rievaulx)

Table of Contents

Preface

Celtic spirituality has been an intellectual interest of mine for years, although, because of my Irish ancestors from County Mayo, it has probably lived deep within me at an unconscious level much longer. I became acquainted with the history of the early Irish church as a graduate student at the University of Notre Dame while researching the ministry of soul friendship for my doctoral dissertation. In 1982, when I visited England and Ireland for the first time with my wife, JoAnne, I was profoundly affected by the rugged beauty of the mountains, forests, lakes, and seashores, the carvings of the saints on the high crosses, and, not least, the friendliness of the people. Since that trip I have taught courses on the history of Celtic Christianity at the College of St. Catherine in St. Paul, Minnesota, given retreats and workshops on Celtic spirituality and soul friendship in parishes and at national conferences, and written extensively on those subjects, especially as they relate to lay leadership. Over the past decade I have also made numerous journeys to important monastic sites in Ireland, England, Scotland, and Wales where the Celtic saints once lived. My appreciation of Celtic history and spirituality has been enriched by the comments and questions of my students, and in unexpected ways my trips abroad have deeply touched both my imagination and my heart. As a result of those experiences, I am acutely aware of the living presence of the past and of our ability even now to communicate with the saints in prayer—and they with us.

As Thomas Merton's *The Wisdom of the Desert* introduced readers to the desert Christians of the third and fourth centuries who acted as spiritual guides, I hope this book will acquaint more people with those spiritual leaders of the early Celtic church who lived from the fifth through the eighth centuries. These men and women were influenced significantly by the earlier stories and ministries of the desert Christians, primarily lay people who lived in Palestine, Syria, and Egypt. While the desert Christians referred to their spiritual guides as *abbas* (fathers) or *ammas* (mothers), the word the early Celtic Christians used to describe their own tradition of spiritual mentors was *anamchara*, Gaelic for "friend of the soul" or simply "soul friend." An *anamchara* is someone with whom we can share our greatest joys and deepest fears, confess our worst sins and most persistent faults, clarify our highest hopes and perhaps most unarticulated dreams. A saying, found in the medieval *Book of Leinster*, attests to the widespread popularity of soul-friendship in the early Celtic church. St. Brigit, Ireland's best-known female saint, is quoted as telling a cleric who visits her regularly that "anyone without a soul friend is like a body without a head." Although this form of ministry was eventually identified in the Roman Catholic church with the ordained priest in the sacrament of reconciliation, in the earliest days of Celtic Christianity such relationships were open to lay people and ordained, women and men alike.

The stories and sayings of the Celtic saints found in this book come from a variety of sources. Some were discovered while I was doing research at the Bodleian Library in Oxford, England, and at St. Patrick's College, Maynooth, Ireland, during a leave of absence from my teaching. Others I have found in various sources since my return to the United States. Stories from two of the Irish women saints' Lives, those of Ita and Samthann, were especially translated for this book by Irish scholars Reverend Diarmuid O'Laoghaire, S.J., and Reverend Peter O'Dwyer, O. Carm., while a colleague, George Rochefort, translated one of the stories of St. Brigit. I am grateful to them for their contribution. Because most of the other Lives were translated in the late nineteenth or early twentieth centuries, I have modernized the translations when appropriate and, of course, edited the selections. Enhanced by the artwork of my friend, Susan McLean-Keeney, I hope they will be conducive to reflection, meditation, and prayer.

This book is dedicated to my students at the College of St. Catherine, who continue to teach me much about women's competence, leadership, and spirituality. It is also dedicated to Thomas Merton, whom I never met in person, but who has inspired me with his writings, the stories of his life, and certain dreams in which he has appeared. In Merton's journal, written a few years before his death in 1968, he writes: "I am reading about Celtic monasticism, the hermits, the lyric poets, the pilgrims, the sea travelers, etc. A whole new world that has waited until now to open up for me."

I hope this book will open up for you, the reader, new horizons too.

Main Celtic
Monastic Sites
Ireland

ULSTER

Derry

Bangor

Glencolumbkille

Nendrum

Downpatrick

Inishmurray

Devenish

Armagh

CONNACHT

Louth

Kells

MEATH

Mayo

Clonbroney

Monasterboice

Clonard

Inisboffin

Anaghdown

Finglas

Clonmacnois

Durrow

Tallaght

Clonfert

Birr

Kildare

Aran Islands

Kilfenora

Saighir

Glendalough

Dysert O'Dea

Scattery Island

Kilkenny

Cashel

Emly

LEINSTER

Ardfert

Killeedy

Lismore

Ferns

Gallerus

MUNSTER

Cork

Gougane Barra

Ardmore

Skellig
Michael

Main Celtic
Monastic Sites
England,
Scotland
and Wales

SCOTLAND

Iona •

Edinburgh
Glasgow •
• Lindisfarne
Melrose

NORTH UMBRIA

Whithorn •
• Whitby

Lastingham

Isle of Man

WALES

Bardsey Island

• St. David's

ENGLAND

• Glastonbury   Canterbury •

CORNWALL

St. Michael's Mount •

Introduction

Sometimes a place holds memories that predate our own personal experiences or recollections. On the banks of the Shannon River in the heart of Ireland stand the ruins of an ancient Celtic monastery that was once one of Ireland's largest, a place of learning and of pilgrimage. Though few trees grow there now, grass colors the site with many shades of green, and, like one of its main rivals, St. Kevin's monastery at Glendalough, it has its share of crosses marking numerous graves. Two large round towers once used as bell-towers to call the monks to prayer and as look-out points to warn them of invading Vikings still stand. Down the road from what was once the men's monastic buildings lie the ruins of the Nuns' Church where centuries ago religious women gathered throughout the day and night to pray. On the grounds of the monastery itself four high crosses, beautifully carved out of stone, attract attention. Though the bright colors of their original paint have long since faded, darkened by the weather and the passage of time, the images on the crosses still tell the story of Jesus and the lives of the Celtic saints.

The most stunning of these crosses stands before the west door of what is left of one of the churches. Called the Cross of the Scriptures because of its depiction of the crucifixion on one side and Christ in his glory on the other, it also shows scenes of a king of Ireland helping the founder of the monastery build the first church, and of reconciliation between two hostile Irish kings, possibly brought about through the ministry of a later abbot.

This is the home of St. Ciaran, one of the earliest founders of Celtic monasticism. The monastery he founded in 545 is Clonmacnois, next to Armagh the most prominent home of religion and culture in the early Irish church. Here missionaries were trained who would take the Christian faith to Britain and continental Europe; here men and women, numbering as many as a thousand, perhaps more, prayed for and ministered to each other for almost six hundred years.

An early story in the *Book of Lismore*, a medieval manuscript, tells of this Ciaran, the son of a chariot-maker, who at an early age leaves his parents in order to learn wisdom. His search for wisdom becomes a lifelong pursuit, and the wisdom he acquires seems to come as a result of his deep friendship with certain spiritual mentors. From his teacher, Finnian of Clonard, Ciaran learns the art of healing and the importance of teaching wisdom to others, beginning with the young daughter of an Irish king. From his spiritual guide Enda he is given the courage to pursue his vocation and to found a church at Clonmacnois. And from his close friend Kevin of Glendalough he receives communion and a final blessing at the time of his early death at thirty-three.

While each of the stories of Ciaran gives us intimations about how wisdom is acquired as well as the importance of spiritual mentors in our lives, one of Ciaran's visits to Enda stands out in its unexpectedly vivid imagery. We are told that at the time Ciaran arrived on Aran Island in Galway Bay where Enda was living, both men beheld the same vision of a great tree growing in the middle of Ireland. This tree, while protecting Ireland, also had its fruit carried across the Irish Sea by birds from around the world which filled its branches. Struck by the vision's force, Ciaran turned to Enda and told him what he had seen. Enda, in turn, interpreted for him the symbolic language of the vision, telling him that the great tree they saw "is you, Ciaran, for you are great in the eyes of God." Enda continued: "All of Ireland will be sheltered by the grace within you, and many people will be fed by your fasting and prayers. So, go in the name of God to the center of the island, and found your church on the banks of a stream."

Anyone who knows Ciaran's story and visits the early Christian site of Clonmacnois can almost feel the powerful presence and holiness of this Celtic saint who, according to that early writing, became recognized as a charismatic leader, gifted teacher, and compassionate soul friend. To walk the winding paths among the ruins, and to stand on the same bank of the Shannon where he once stood is to encounter firsthand the wisdom of those early Celtic saints, a wisdom rooted in their spirituality.

This book is about the wisdom of the Celtic saints, those inspired pioneers of the early Celtic church who helped the Christian faith take root and flourish in Ireland and the British Isles. Like Ciaran, many of them were founders of monasteries, which became religious, cultural, and educational centers for leaders, both clerical and lay, during the early Middle Ages. Others travelled as missionaries and pilgrims throughout the world, bringing Christianity not only to the continent of Europe, but possibly to North America as well—centuries before Columbus. All of them were teachers, confessors, and soul friends to countless numbers of people.

One of the main sources that sheds light on Celtic spirituality and soul friendship are the stories and sayings that appear in the *acta sanctorum* or Lives of the Saints. These Lives of the Celtic saints were primarily compiled in the high medieval period (thirteenth to sixteenth centuries), but many were written in the sixth through ninth centuries. Almost all have primitive material that take us back to the earliest days of the Celtic church. As such, they are part of the history of Christian hagiography, a particular genre of literature written to present the saints as worthy spiritual mentors who can inspire us and whose admirable qualities we might integrate into our own personalities and lives. Though not historically accurate biographies as we understand that term today, they do express the larger truths of the saints' lives, the truths that moved them (and can move us) toward greater self-awareness and self-acceptance, wholeness and holiness, meaning and God.

In order for the reader to more fully understand and appreciate the stories and sayings of the early Celtic saints, it is helpful briefly to consider the history of the early Celtic church and specific characteristics of its spirituality as well as examine the religious pattern that underlies many of the stories and the symbolic language they contain. Finally, before turning to the stories and sayings themselves, a specific approach to reading them will be discussed. All of this, I hope, will better prepare the reader for grasping and beginning to integrate Celtic wisdom today.

The Early Celtic Church

Long before theological and political conflicts tragically divided Christianity, one of its most ancient and creative churches grew to prominence. This Celtic church existed from the fifth through the twelfth centuries. During its time it kept classical learning alive while the so-called Dark Ages were casting their shadows across Europe. The Celtic church was made up of a great variety of churches in such places as northern England, Cornwall, Wales, Scotland, Brittany, the Isle of Man, and of course, all of Ireland. Although these churches were never united administratively into one externally visible church, they experienced a large measure of unity among themselves through their monastic lifestyle, friendship among the early saints, respect for women's gifts, and common spirituality. This Celtic Christian spirituality was very much the child of the pagan culture which preceded it, one that valued poetic imagination and artistic creativity, kinship relations and the warmth of a hearth, the wonder of stories and the guidance of dreams. It was a spirituality profoundly affected by the beauty of the landscape, the powerful presence of the sea, and the swift passage at night of the full moon across open skies. Baptized in the waters of Christian faith by such leaders as Patrick, Brigit, and Columcille (Ireland's "holy trinity" of saints), this pagan spirituality eventually flowered into monastic cities, high crosses, illuminated gospels, and a ministry of spiritual mentoring that changed profoundly the course of Christian spirituality.

No one knows precisely when the Christian faith arrived in Ireland and the British Isles, but there are a number of fascinating legends about the spread of Christianity to that part of the world. Some say that either St. Peter or St. Paul travelled to Britain and established the church there; others tell how Joseph of Arimathea, who had cared for the body of Christ, came to Glastonbury, England, and planted a thorn from Christ's head near a small church in sight of the famous Tor. Besides these legends there are stories about the Celtic saints who lived, worked, and prayed in Ireland and the British Isles. Although details about the earliest of them are historically vague, these latter tales bring us closer to the geographical and spiritual landscape of the early Celtic church. Ninian is said to have founded a monastery, *Candida Casa* (the White House), at Whithorn in southern Scotland in 397. This monastery became an important place for educating missionaries and laity. Patrick is credited with bringing the Christian faith to Ireland in 432, but there were probably Christians living on that island years before his arrival. In 596 Augustine, the first archbishop of Canterbury, was sent by Pope Gregory the Great to evangelize the people in southern England, while northern England came under the influence of missionaries from Iona. Between the fifth and eighth centuries Wales was Christianized by wandering monks and missionaries.

The sixth century especially saw the rise of the great monasteries in Ireland and the Celtic parts of the British Isles. These monasteries were headed by powerful abbesses or abbots, such as Brigit of Kildare, Columcille of Iona, Finnian of Clonard,

Ita of Killeedy, Brendan of Clonfert, Kevin of Glendalough, Ciaran of Clonmacnois, and David of Wales. Many of the first male founders and abbots of these monasteries, as the early hagiographies maintain, were probably celibate priests and bishops. Women founders and abbesses also lived celibate lives within religious communities. This way of life was chosen because of the value the early church placed on virginity, in imitation of Christ. For women in particular, the monastic life offered the opportunity to develop intellectual abilities and creative pursuits. It was the only alternative to the roles of wife and mother in marriage, or, in spinsterhood, that of maintaining a household for aging parents and unmarried siblings. The male monastic leaders who followed the early pioneers might have been either ordained or lay. Many were evidently married, since the marriage of priests throughout the entire early church was commonplace and the Celtic church was no exception. In some Irish monasteries, in fact, the abbacy descended from father to son.

By the seventh century a distinct form of Christianity had emerged in Ireland and the British Isles. While there was much diversity within the universal church from its earliest days—differences rooted in racial, cultural, and historical developments which affected the leadership of the local churches and their understanding of Christianity—the early Celtic church was unique. Influenced greatly by the values of the Celtic pagan culture that preceded the arrival of Christianity on its shores, as well as the ideals of the early desert Christians who valued simplicity of life and the equality of all in the eyes of God, this Celtic church frequently found itself in conflict with other churches, including the church in Rome, over issues specifically related to church governance and sexuality.

Many of the other Western churches, adopting the social structures of the declining Roman Empire as their own, divided church territory into dioceses, headed by bishops who lived primarily in urban areas. The early Celtic church, however, was located more often in rural or remote areas and influenced by the tribal system of the pagan Celts. Monastic leaders who emerged at the great Celtic monasteries were eventually more powerful than the bishops who lived in their midst. Even when leadership was limited to celibates or the ordained, the monasteries themselves had many lay people (known as *manaigh*) attached to them.

Celibate members within the monastic communities as well as these lay people experienced the fruits of collaboration. Education, pastoral care, and liturgical leadership were provided by the monks or religious women; in turn, lay people and their families helped the monasteries grow their crops, manage their farms, fish, plant trees, and keep their bees. All benefited from this mutual sharing of gifts, including those who only came for a short stay. As one of the earliest hagiographers, Cogitosus, writes about those who visited the monastery of St. Brigit at Kildare: "Who can list the chaotic crowds and countless folk who flock in from all the provinces: some for the abundance of food, others who are feeble seeking health, others just to look at the mobs, and still others who come with great gifts to the festival of Saint Brigit."

Differences between Roman-style and Celtic churches also emerged over time as the Roman Empire was broken apart by invading Germanic tribes, including the Anglo-Saxons who swept into Britain in the fifth century, driving many Celts back into those geographical areas now identified as Scotland, Wales, and Cornwall. While other ecclesial bodies came to value large churches and basilicas for their communal liturgies, the Celtic church built small ones of wood and, later, stone. Even when the membership in the monasteries increased, the Celtic Christians, wanting to maintain greater intimacy among their members, continued to build more numerous and smaller church dwellings rather than larger structures for worship. Also, as the continental churches grew increasingly more materialistic, dressing their bishops in fine vestments and having them ride on golden thrones (as described in the *Life of Wilfrid*, a Northumbrian saint), the Celtic church valued a more ascetic lifestyle. Inspired by the stories of the desert father St. Antony (251-356) and of the anchorite bishop of Tours, St. Martin (316-97), the Celtic church was characterized by intense missionary outreach, a pastoral ministry among the common people, and leaders who ate sparsely and spent long hours in prayer, sometimes immersed nightly in the ocean's frigid waters. The early Celtic monastic bishops themselves, such as David of Wales and Aidan of Lindisfarne, dressed simply, clad in coarse robes, usually carrying with them on their pastoral visits only a walking-stick and a bell, which, as they approached, would be rung loudly to alert the local people. (Celestine, bishop of Rome in the early fifth century did not appreciate what he called their "innovation" in dress. He condemned the appointment of Celtic "wanderers and strangers" over the local clergy in Gaul who "clad in a cloak, and with a girdle round the loins" are "changing the usage of so many years, of such great prelates, for another [type of] habit.")

Differences between the churches related to sexuality arose. While the other Christian churches increasingly isolated women from positions of authority and relationships of friendship with males, the Celtic church, influenced by the pagan Celts' belief that women were equal to men and had similar legal rights, encouraged their leadership. Contrary to the prevailing dualistic tendencies found among desert Christians and the inhabitants of countries bordering the Mediterranean, the early founders of the Celtic church "did not reject," according to a ninth-century manuscript, *Catalogue of the Saints in Ireland*, "the service and society of women." Women were valued and not ignored, judging from one of the earliest Irish martyrologies, that of Gorman, which lists over two hundred female saints. Monastic communities, which arose in Ireland shortly after the death of Patrick in 461, were also headed by women. The oldest monasteries of women recorded in Ireland are those of Brigit of Kildare, Moninne at Killeavy, and Ita at Killeedy.

Many of these women leaders held powerful ecclesial positions in communities consisting of both women and men. These "double monasteries" were evidently a normal feature of the earliest monastic life in Ireland and England. The most well-known abbesses over these double monasteries were Brigit, who founded a community at Kildare, Ireland, and Hild of Whitby, Northumbria. (Hild, of Anglo-Saxon origins, received her religious formation from Aidan of Lindisfarne and was, as we will see, very much affected by and in sympathy with the Celtic monks and their spirituality.) The origins of these double monasteries of monks and nuns is unclear although Cogitosus, the seventh-century biographer of Brigit, describes the one at Kildare as a double monastery that must have originated at least one hundred years before he wrote. There the monks and nuns lived in separate quarters, but worshipped together in a common church in which the lay people joined them for liturgies. Double monasteries were quite numerous in England during the seventh century. We know of such establishments at Coldingham, Ely, Repton, Barking,

Bardney, Wimborne (Dorset), and Wenlock. The Roman-appointed Theodore of Tarsus did not initially approve of this feature of the Celtic and Anglo-Saxon churches, but accepted it as the custom of the land when he arrived at Canterbury in 669 to become archbishop—after a plague had wiped out most of the English episcopate. The early biographies of Brigit, as well as the stories of Hild, show clearly that such powerful abbesses exercised an influence on their times that has almost no parallel in later history—except perhaps for Hildegard of Bingen in the twelfth century and Teresa of Avila in the sixteenth. Unfortunately, most of those double monasteries were destroyed by the Vikings in the ninth century when they laid waste to so many of the Celtic church's monasteries and artistic treasures.

Another area related to sexuality in the early Celtic church—the Celtic missionaries close ministerial association with women—met with vehement condemnations from church authorities on the continent. Judging from protests against the practice, missionaries evidently travelled quite frequently with women companions, some of whom helped with the celebration of the eucharist. According to a sixth-century letter written by bishops in Gaul to Irish missionaries:

> Through a report made by the venerable Sparatus, we have learned that you continually carry around from one of your fellow-countrymen's huts to another, certain tables upon which you celebrate the divine sacrifice of the Mass, assisted by women whom you call conhospitae; and while you distribute the eucharist, they take the chalice and administer the blood of Christ to the people. This is an innovation, an unheard-of superstition. . . . For the love of Christ, and in the name of the Church United and of our common faith, we beg you to renounce immediately upon receipt of this letter, these abuses of the table. . . . We appeal to your charity, not only to restrain these little women from staining the holy sacraments by administering them illicitly, but also not to admit to live under your roof any woman who is not your grandmother, your mother, your sister, or your niece.

Although tensions between the two forms of Christianity eventually led to open disagreements at the Synod of Whitby in 664 over such issues as when Easter should be celebrated and what form of tonsure or hairstyle should be worn by the ordained, these other differences, intimately related to each other's concept of church, ministerial leadership, and spirituality, were far more important. They ultimately resulted in the submersion of the Celtic church in Ireland by the Roman ecclesial system in the twelfth century.

Still, despite that "reform," which was a triumph for ecclesial administrators but a tragedy for Irish culture and creativity, Celtic Christian spirituality survived in various geographical locations where the saints had once lived or journeyed. It deeply affected directly or indirectly certain religious traditions and wisdom figures, including Hildegard of Bingen, Francis of Assisi, Julian of Norwich, Joan of Arc, George Herbert, Evelyn Underhill, and Thomas Merton. In many ways this Celtic spirituality is the foundation of Anglican, Episcopalian, and Methodist spirituality, and, because of its love of the desert fathers and mothers, it has a great affinity with the spirituality of the Eastern Orthodox. With its focus upon nature and the entire spiritual realm, and its respect for ancestors, visions, and dreams, it finds resonance with Native American spirituality too. Thus, the spirituality of the Christian Celts has great ecumenical value, for it transcends the differences which have divided Christians in the East and the West since before the Reformation. It also has special appeal for many of us today who are concerned about the ecological survival of our planet, the revitalization of our churches, and the quality of our own spiritual life.

This Celtic Christian spirituality is especially reflected in the hagiographies of the saints. Within their stories and sayings we will be able to discern key characteristics of that spirituality, which we may want to integrate into our own lives and ministries.

Celtic Spirituality

One of the primary characteristics of the early Celtic Christians was their love of and respect for the physical environment. Their daily life was lived in close proximity to nature, and their spirituality reflected what the Welsh call *hud*: a sense of wonder and awe at the divine residing in everything. Their pagan ancestors, like other primitive peoples, had a deep respect for nature, regarding the earth as a mother, the source of all fertility. Their spiritual leaders, the druids and druidesses, believed that the supernatural pervaded every aspect of life and that spirits were everywhere: in ancient trees and sacred groves, mountaintops and rock formations, rivers, streams, and holy wells. Influenced by that pagan spiritual heritage, Celtic Christians found it natural to address God as "Lord of the Elements," and to experience communion with God in their natural surroundings. In the stories of the saints, they are often found establishing their monasteries and oratories in places where the druids and druidesses had once taught and worshipped—in the midst of oak groves or near sacred springs, on the shores of secluded lakes, or on misty islands far out at sea.

This attitude of deep respect for the environment was also manifest in their quiet care for all living things. As we will see, the Celtic saints seem to have had a special affinity and reciprocal relationship with animals: Kevin shelters in his hands a blackbird which probably sang for him; Ciaran meets a wild boar that helps him clear land for his monastery; Columcille's white horse sheds great tears at his master's approaching death. Animals are portrayed as fellow creatures of the earth, and once befriended, they become helpers to the saints.

A second characteristic inherited from their druidic mentors was their love of learning. Christian Ireland in particular was the place where monastic schools flourished and where the original pagan Celtic legends and stories of the saints were first written down in the monastic scriptoria. According to the great storyteller Bede the Venerable (c. 672-735), many pilgrim scholars came to Ireland from Britain and the continent of Europe to study and learn:

> In the course of time some of these devoted themselves faithfully to the monastic life, while others preferred to travel round to the cells of various teachers and apply themselves to study. The Irish welcomed them all gladly, gave them their daily food, and also provided them with books to read and with instruction, without asking for any payment.

Inspired, surely, by the teachers and tutors they encountered living in those cells, visitors must have learned a great deal about holiness and God. We can see this respect for study and yearning for wisdom in the frequent references to books in the hagiographies of the early Celtic saints. We also find those characteristics in specific stories; for example, in Aidan's encouraging all those who travelled with him to study for some time each day, and in Columcille's spending so much time alone in his cell to study and write. Irish missionaries, like Columban (c. 543-615), brought this love of learning to France, Switzerland, Germany, and Italy, where they founded other great monastic schools that kept Celtic wisdom alive for generations after the deaths of the original saintly pioneers.

A third characteristic associated with the early Christian Celts and revealed in their stories is their innate yearning to explore the unknown. Perhaps this wanderlust was due to the migratory nature of their pagan ancestors, who in the third century B.C.E. had been the dominant race of all of Europe; perhaps it was their living in such close proximity to the sea and the natural rhythm of its tides; perhaps their Judeo-Christian spiritual heritage unconsciously inspired them with its own stories of Jonah in the belly of the whale, of Abraham and Sarah's travel to a foreign land, of Moses' exodus out of Egypt, and of Peter's and Paul's missionary journeys. Whatever the reason, many of them shared the desire to travel and, in contrast to the "red martyrdom" of giving one's life up for Christ or the "green martyrdom" of participating in severe penitential practices, they faced the "white martyrdom" of living years far from home and hearth for the sake of the gospels. (The Celts had a specific word, *hiraeth*, for the extreme yearning for home associated with this latter form of martyrdom; because of their deep love of family, it was considered the hardest of all to endure.) Beginning with St. Patrick, Celtic missionaries (called *peregrini*) chose this way of life out of deep devotion to Christ, but also perhaps because of their genuine appreciation of God's mysterious creation and their own desire to see the holy places and meet people different than themselves.

Whatever the reasons for their travel, the theme of pilgrimage is one of the key elements of the early saints' spirituality. For them, to make a journey for Christ brought—despite the hardships—unexpected blessings, increased intimacy with God, and the healing of body and soul. Brendan the Navigator is, of course, the most famous of these pilgrims, but there are others as well. Each saint is profoundly affected by his or her journeys and returns with new experiences and wisdom to share with those who remained at home. A chain of mentoring is formed, and, as we will see in Kevin's story in particular, the monasteries the early saints founded and the tombs where their bodies are placed for the Day of Resurrection become, in turn, important sites to which others journey on pilgrimage.

A fourth characteristic of Celtic spirituality is the Celtic Christians' love of silence and of solitude. Considering the widespread travel of so many *peregrini* and the extensive pastoral work of all the Celtic saints, it is intriguing and somewhat paradoxical how much the early Christian Celts also valued solitary places and times of silence. An atmosphere of silence was encouraged within their monasteries and certain quiet times were strictly observed—as we find in the stories of David of Wales. Perhaps they sought out places of solitude precisely because of their intense involvement with people.

Many of the Celtic monasteries also had a place apart—a cell, retreat, or *dysert*—in which a monk or nun could retire when he or she needed to be alone. Sometimes the Celtic saints chose a cave for shelter and reflection, as did Columban and Ninian of Whithorn (362-432). Others moved to a hill or mountaintop to fast and pray. Many, as is clear in the stories of Aidan, Columcille, and Cuthbert, seemed especially drawn to be near the ocean's waves. Whatever their reasons for treasuring silence and seeking the solitary life, the early Christian Celts shared what the scholar John Ryan calls a "surprising" combination of "apostolic and anchoretical ideals."

A fifth characteristic of Celtic spirituality has to do with their understanding of time. The early saints appreciated time as a sacred reality blessed and *already* redeemed by God's overflowing compassion. This awareness of the sacred dimension to time is not the same as modern Western culture's frantic preoccupation in which "every minute counts." Rather, the Celts' perception was that there is a fullness *now* to all of time, manifest in the old Irish saying, "When God made time, he made plenty of it." With this perception of time as a gift from God, time in a chronological sense (with one historical event following another) was disregarded by the early Celts. For them, the present contains within itself both past events, which continue to live on, as well as the seeds of future events waiting to be born.

Without clear demarcations between past, present, and future, Celtic Christians interpreted history differently than we do. They made contemporaries of those who historically could never have been. In some of the early legends, for example, Brigit and

---

24

Ita are portrayed as midwives to Mary, the mother of Jesus. As soul friends they help bring Jesus to birth and they nurse him. In certain stories Brigit and Patrick are described as intimate friends—when in fact they probably never met. (If the traditional dates of their lives are relied upon, Brigit would have been about six years old at the time of Patrick's death.) That did not matter to the early Christian Celts, for, from their point of view, people with the qualities and holiness of Patrick and Brigit would naturally be friends—even if they lived at different times in the chronological sequence of history.

In many ways Celtic Christians saw the larger truths of myth and the lasting effects of relationships of love standing outside of time, having an eternal quality that certainly cannot be understood fully by considering chronological time alone. The early Celts also believed in "thin places": geographical locations scattered throughout Ireland and the British Isles where a person experiences only a very thin divide between past, present, and future times; places where a person is somehow able, possibly only for a moment, to encounter a more ancient reality within present time; or places where perhaps only in a glance we are somehow transported into the future. Some of the stories here that associate the saints with intuitive and psychic powers attest to these "thin places." Other stories of certain saints who communicate with each other after the death of one of them, such as Ciaran and Kevin, and Maedoc and Columcille, affirm the existence not only of "thin places" but also of bonds of soul friendship, which death itself can never destroy.

A sixth characteristic of Celtic spirituality, related to their concept of time, was the Celtic Christians' appreciation of ordinary life. Recognizing time as a reality made holy by a loving God, the Celtic saints valued the daily, the routine, the ordinary. They believed God is found not so much at the end of time when the reign of God *finally* comes, but *now*, where the reign is already being lived by God's faithful people. Theirs was a spirituality characterized by gratitude, and in our stories we find them worshipping God in their daily work and very ordinary chores.

Another quality, their joy, is apparent in the last words of David of Wales to his friends: "My brothers and sisters, be joyful, keep your faith and belief, and perform the small things which you have learned from me and have seen in me." Seeing their daily lives as revelatory of God's love, they valued the cyclical dimension of time, believing that by immersing themselves in the seasons of the year and uniting their lives with the liturgical seasons of the church, they could more effectively celebrate time's sacredness as well as their own sacred journeys through time. This perception is especially evident in the stories of St. Brendan of Clonfert, which tell how he and his crew celebrated feasts, such as Easter and Christmas, in a certain way and at the same places each year. Daily routines and yearly observances, the Christian Celts believed, are not boring. Rather, they can help us realize the immanence of God in time and the inherent holiness of our lives when we immerse ourselves in God's time.

A seventh characteristic of the spirituality of Celtic Christians was their belief in the great value of kinship relationships, especially the spiritual ties of soul friends. The pagan Celts in Ireland and throughout Europe valued their families and their tribal affiliations. They developed a fosterage system in which children of one family were brought up by another family or tribe. They believed that such exchanges not only strengthened alliances but introduced each child to a wider world of learning. The pagan Celts' druids and druidesses also acted as teachers of the tribes and advisers to the kings. Like Native American shamans, they functioned as mediators between the tribes and the spiritual realm: the world of tribal gods, goddesses, and spirits. These types of mentoring relationships survived when Christianity arrived.

The hagiographies tell numerous stories about younger people being guided and educated by the Celtic saints at their monasteries or cells. As the story of Ciaran of Clonmacnois and his mentor Enda shows, each of the early saints seems to have had at least one personal mentor, a wiser, more experienced, sometimes older teacher, confessor, or spiritual guide. (Holiness, not age, seems to be a more important criterion of such a person, as we will see in a story about St. Findbarr). This soul friend was not necessarily male or ordained. Some of the greatest and most well-known of the soul friends in the early Celtic church were women, such as abbesses Ita, Brigit, Samthann, and Hild. Not only were these women teachers, administrators, guides, preachers, and confessors who, as in the stories of Ita, did not hesitate to give out penances, but at least two of them, according to early hagiographies, had in their possession religious articles traditionally associated with a bishop. Brigit, in Cogitosus's Life, receives a pallium (a bishop's mantle), and in a later hagiography, she is said to have been ordained; Samthann had a marvelous crozier (a bishop's staff), which was able to perform miracles.

Besides human soul friends, female and male, many of the saints had angelic ones. Christian Celts believed in the existence of these invisible guides, whose leader was identified as the archangel Michael or, in Patrick's case, as Victor. Manifestations of God's care, these angels seem to appear at crucial turning points in the lives of the saints. They baptize the saints, name them, appear in their dreams, help them discern their vocations, and lead them to the sites of their monasteries and eventually to their own places of resurrection.

The stories and sayings of the Celtic saints clearly reveal that mentoring and spiritual guidance were considered an important if not essential part of Celtic Christian spirituality. All the saints seem to have been changed profoundly by these relationships—whether their mentors were human or angelic, and whether they offered a compassionate ear or a challenging word. They were keenly aware, as are many today, that inner healing happens when we openly and honestly acknowledge to another person our concerns, grief, and spiritual diseases, and that God is very close to those who speak as friends do, heart to heart. While other characteristics of Celtic spirituality can be found in the stories of the saints—such as their valuing dreams as sources of spiritual wisdom, and their love of storytelling, good music, poetry, and dance—one of the greatest discoveries of the Christian Celts, according to scholar Nora Chadwick, is "the range and significance of individual experience, and the interest and the humor of little things, and how exciting and valuable it is to share them with one another." This, of course, is what many would equate with the value and joy of having a soul friend, a person with whom we can share the significant and often insignificant experiences of our lives and discover, often in the telling, that the seemingly insignificant events are really the most important of all, the times when and places where God speaks.

Spiritual Kinship With Jesus

Anyone who reads the Lives of the Celtic saints will soon recognize that each saint is portrayed not only as an extraordinary person, but above all as an *imago Christi*, that is, as a living symbol or image of Christ. This way of identifying a saint, of course, is nothing new in the history of Christian spirituality, for from the beginning of Christian life, each of us, through baptism, is welcomed into a community and hopefully begins to integrate in a lifelong process the significant values, attributes, and perspectives associated with Jesus himself.

Although many of the Celtic hagiographies were inspired by and some of the contents borrowed wholesale from other earlier writings, such as Athanasius's *Life of Antony*, Cassian's *Conferences*, and Sulpicius Severus's *Life of St. Martin* (of Tours), the ultimate Christian literary source for all of them were the gospel stories. We thus find the Celtic saints doing in their time with their contemporaries what Jesus did in his: healing the sick, feeding the hungry, praying in solitude, having intimate friendships with both women and men, calming the sea, even raising the dead. Like Jesus' story, the future significance and shape of their lives are sometimes announced in extraordinary predictions and dreams. Like him, their ministries are filled with tension, conflict, and times of grief and despair.

Overall, when one considers the stories of the Celtic saints found in these early Lives, a pattern can be discerned similar to the one found in Jesus' life and ministry. It is this pattern that lies behind many of the stories of the Celtic saints in this book.

The **first stage** in a saint's Life usually begins with mention of the saint's distinguished ancestry and with descriptions of how the saint's birth was preceded by extraordinary events and prophetic dreams. As in the opening chapters of the gospels of Matthew and Luke, which describe Jesus' conception and birth, Brigit's birth, for example, is foretold by a druid, Brendan's mother has a vision in which her breasts shine like snow, Columcille's mother dreams of a cloak of many colors, and Findbarr, while yet in his mother's womb, cries out to the king to spare his parents from destruction. Certain holy people are also often present shortly after the birth of the saint to confirm the newborn's future greatness—similar to the story in Luke in which the elderly Simeon and the prophetess Anna prophesy to Joseph and Mary when they bring Jesus as a child to the Temple (Lk 2:22-38).

A **second stage** occurs when the saint finds a worthy mentor or mentors, human or angelic, from whom wisdom is learned. In the gospel of Mark, Jesus went to John the Baptist, received affirmation from the Spirit of God at his baptism, and was cared for by angels after his temptations in the wilderness. Mention has already been made of the vast networks of friendships among the Celtic saints and the mentoring they received from childhood on. In the stories which follow, some of the most outstanding examples reflecting this second stage are the guidance Ciaran receives from Finnian and Enda, Brendan from Ita, Hild from Aidan, and Cuthbert from Boisil. The Celtic saints also receive help from angels and animals, who act as their guides.

A **third stage** in the stories of the saints recounts becoming a spiritual leader or mentor for others after the saint has experienced transformation and grown in spiritual wisdom. In the gospels Jesus, after leaving the wilderness in which he has confronted his own demons, calls his first disciples at the Sea of Galilee (Mk 1:16 ff.) and then proceeds to gather a group of both women and men around him in order to teach them what he knows. So also with the Celtic saints. Though varying in degrees of enthusiasm (Kevin of Glendalough, for one, wants to be left alone), each of the saints—sometimes early in adult life, sometimes later in maturity—eventually attracts a following, builds a monastery, and offers guidance to those who come for help.

A **fourth stage** in the stories of the saints tells of their miracles, which demonstrate their spiritual power and intimacy with God. These worthy and miraculous deeds frequently take the form of Jesus' miracles, such as healing the sick, casting out demons, multiplying food, and changing water into wine. (The Celtic saints, such as Brigit, however, seem to prefer beer to wine!) The numerous references to miraculous deeds show that miracles are not dependent so much upon the saints' own abilities as upon their compassion—and upon their crying out in prayer to a merciful, all-powerful God. The underlying theological lesson is this: it is important to unite our life with God's, and all sorts of amazing things happen when we do.

29

A **fifth stage** in the saints' lives involves traveling to other parts of the country (as Jesus did throughout his public ministry and on his journey to Jerusalem) or to foreign shores. The Celtic saints whose stories appear in this book frequently visit each other's monasteries to teach, to learn, or just to renew old friendships. They also travel abroad to visit Christian holy places or to bring Christianity to those who have not yet heard the Good News. Some, like Findbarr, Kevin, and Maedoc, go to Rome, while others, like Aidan, Brendan, Non, and Ia, walk to distant peoples or sail to unknown shores. David of Wales, according to his hagiographer, even went to Jerusalem where he was consecrated bishop.

A **sixth stage** that appears in many hagiographies relates that the saints seem to intuit the approach of their death. The Celtic saints consistently prepare their followers for their departure, and sometimes, despite their own fear of dying, they seem to offer those who will be left behind more comfort than they themselves receive. Many of the saints impart final words of wisdom as a sacred legacy—much as Jesus did at the Last Supper and on the cross. This intuition about approaching death is expressed in the stories when a saint is forewarned by a divine visitor or when an angel leads the saint to his or her true place of resurrection. Some of the most moving stories in this book are those describing the deaths of the saints and what they tell their followers before—or sometimes after—they have died.

Finally, a **seventh stage** can be perceived in the miracles and marvelous happenings that occur after the death of the beloved saint. Fire, for example, appears at Patrick's tomb; a violent storm is calmed after the death of Columcille; the sun shines for twelve days straight when Findbarr dies. These accounts are similar to those events originally associated with the death of Jesus when the veil of the Temple was torn in two, the earth quaked, rocks split, and the dead rose from their graves (Mt 27:51 ff.). As in the stories of Jesus' resurrection, the dead saints appear to their friends, sometimes in dreams or in visions in which their souls are seen to be carried to heaven. Cures occur at their tombs. Although unusual phenomena, Christian Celts hearing these stories did not find them at all unbelievable; they were very much convinced that the faithful dead were truly still alive. They also knew from their own experiences that God works in mysterious ways. They accepted that people sometimes do know intuitively of deaths or are healed unexpectedly at graves; that nature itself sometimes manifests its unity with humankind by sending signs that it recognizes the passing of those who have led holy lives.

These seven stages make up a pattern that reflects each saint's spiritual kinship with Jesus. All of them, by uniting their hearts and minds with Jesus, were changed profoundly by him and his story. By implication, this pattern suggested to the readers of those hagiographies that their own spirituality was meant to be shaped, as the saints' lives were, by Jesus. This pattern can be discerned in many of the stories of the Celtic saints in this book, though the stages do not necessarily follow in the order outlined. These stages are not always apparent in the Lives of the female saints, because many of their stories are fragmentary or incomplete, appearing in the hagiographies of male saints rather than in their own. Tragically, few of the women's monasteries were wealthy enough to be able to afford a hagiographer, while others, because of their size, were the first to be destroyed by the invading Vikings. Their stories, like so many women's stories today, need to be recovered and retold for the tremendous wisdom they contain.

Symbols and Sacred Numbers

Besides the religious pattern the hagiographers used to represent the saints' paths to holiness and spiritual wisdom, we find that other sides of the saints' personalities appear in these early stories. At times the saints seem to be living according to a different standard than that of the Sermon on the Mount. In some of the legends about Patrick, for example, he curses his enemies, especially the druids, and in other ways attacks and punishes those who are opposed to him. Other monastic founders, voyagers, and missionaries sometimes employ similar means to maintain their claims against each other or to vanquish their foes. These stories reveal the influence of the earlier pagan culture and its own understanding of what constitutes a genuine hero.

According to the pagan Celts, heroes, both male and female, were people of great physical beauty with unusual magical powers, including the ability to change shapes and even to transcend space and time. They also were flesh-and-blood individuals not only filled with human idealism but susceptible to human error. These heroes had strange visions, made voyages to other worlds, travelled in company with friends, and endured great hardships for the tribe. Once the monks of the monasteries in the seventh, eighth, and ninth centuries began to write down their remembrances of the early saints, they naturally presented them in a guise that the Celtic people would expect of their heroes. Thus, certain saints are portrayed as having the virtues of a warrior—strength, loyalty, and bravery. Practices such as boasting and cursing were also included in their descriptions of what the saints said and did.

Since the early hagiographers saw little difference between ordinary tales and religious ones, they often blended the two. Frequently hagiographers incorporated into the Lives of the saints certain folktales that were popular at the time they wrote. Traces of these folktales appear in the stories of Brendan's voyage to the Promised Land; Brigit's talented fox at the court of an Irish king; David's marvelous horse, which Findbarr rode across the Irish Sea; and Kevin's encounter with a fairy-witch.

Celtic hagiography is full of mythic components, the language of folktales, fairy tales, and dreams. This language, related closely to the transforming power of symbols, was not used to deceive or to mislead readers of the hagiographies, but rather to provide them with intimations of the saint's greatness and assurances that each saint was especially loved, protected, and guided by God. Certain symbols and sacred numbers were used in the stories to enhance the saint's heroic reputation. The most significant symbols are these:

Animals and Birds

Joseph Campbell says that early tribes, living so close to nature, highly respected and revered animals and birds as "tutors of humanity." They were identified with specific qualities and adopted as tribal totems and personal mentors. They symbolize our intuitive powers and helping instincts; to befriend them or to allow them to befriend us is to be guided by those powers and instincts. Among the pagan Celts both wild and domestic animals were relied upon for food, clothing, transportation, and warmth. Animals of the hunt such as stags, boars, and bears are frequently depicted in art, while hunting itself was a ritual activity in which tribes called upon certain animals for their protection. Celtic literature is filled with references to birds, which were understood to be intermediaries between this world and the otherworld.

Certain birds such as the owl and the dove were considered to have oracular abilities and prophetic powers. (This is clear in one of the stories of Brendan, who is guided on his voyage by a bird who speaks to him.) The Celts were aware of the important contribution to human life of nature's creatures, and that is behind the many references to animals and birds in the Lives of the Celtic saints. The more common animals and birds, along with their symbolic meaning, are the following:

Bee: A primary symbol of wisdom, bees were known for their industry in producing honey, one of the foods of the Promised Land. They were believed to be special creatures who took an acute interest in the affairs of their owners. If a bee entered a house it was considered a good omen. In his hagiography of Ninian of Whithorn, Aelred of Rievaulx compares the saint to a bee: "Like a bee he formed for himself the honeycombs of wisdom." Before the birth of David of Wales a symbol of his future wisdom, a honeycomb, appears to his father.

Boar: A symbol of strength and power, the boar was adopted by the Celts as an image of war because of its ferocity. It is found on surviving warrior helmets and armor. The boar also symbolized prosperity, because pork was a favorite Celtic food and played an important part in feasting. In the story of Kevin, he protects a wild boar, thus showing his respect for all of creation and perhaps for the wildest elements in himself.

Cow: Because of the necessity of milk for sustenance and nourishment in early agricultural societies, a cow was considered to have quasi-mystical powers. Among Celts it had great social value. There are numerous references in early and medieval literature concerning wars and cattle raids. In the stories of the saints, Brigit's mother is a milkmaid and her newborn child is washed in milk, symbolizing Brigit's special character. Ciaran takes a white cow with him to Clonard. Her hide has miraculous powers, representing Ciaran's own intimacy with God. Samthann is said to never have had more than six cows, a reference to her deliberate decision to remain poor.

Crane: In cultures ranging from the Chinese to those of the Mediterranean, the crane is a symbol of justice, longevity, and diligence. In Irish sagas cranes represent women and, because of their association with water, transformation as well. It is significant that Columcille was called "the crane-cleric," and that he welcomed a poor crane with tenderness and kindness to Iona, possibly representing his love for his own feminine side.

Dove: A bird identified with the ability to speak of future happenings and to act as a guide to the spiritual realm, the dove represented inspiration and spirituality for many early peoples. In Christianity, of course, it is a symbol of the Holy Spirit. Hagiographers, such as those of Brigit, Columcille, and David, used the dove in their stories to show how truly inspired and holy their saints were, with talents in preaching and teaching.

Fox: A symbol of cleverness and ingenuity, the fox is the most frequent actor in folktales. It was often depicted as having the ability to outsmart other animals, although not always domestic animals, such as the cat. Foxes appear in the earliest hagiographies, including those of Patrick and Brigit.

Horse: The horse, a symbol of fertility, sanctity, strength, speed, and sexual vigor, appears on many ancient Celtic coins. Horses were and are revered by the Celts and were crucial to the Celtic way of life in a warrior society. Horses were especially associated with prestige and nobility. For Aidan of Lindisfarne to give his horse away was an important symbolic act of renunciation and humility; for Columcille to be mourned by a horse represented his own noble and saintly character.

Otter: A creature at home in two elements, land and water, the otter symbolized the union of the spiritual and natural realms. In Irish folklore otters were associated with omniscience, for Celts believed that otters slept with their eyes open and thus did not miss anything. It is significant that Kevin, the Irish saint, and Cuthbert, the Northumbrian saint, both have friendly otters as helpmates.

Salmon: The salmon as a symbol of wisdom figures into both Celtic sagas and saints' lives. According to the story of the hero Fionn Mac Cumhaill, nine magic hazel trees, containing all of the world's wisdom, grew on the banks of the pool of Fec, at the source of the river Boyne. The salmon of the pool, feeding on the nuts, stored that wisdom in themselves. By eating one of those fish Fionn acquired his magical knowledge of the otherworld. Among the stories of Brendan, we find the saint discovering salmon in the Land of Promise. In the account of Kevin, his community is threatened when one of the monks tries to kill the otter that brings salmon to it each night.

Stag: For hunters, the stag with its tree-like antlers symbolized the spirit of the forest, fertility, and virility. Because of the autumn shedding and spring growth of its antlers, reflecting the falling and reappearance of leaves on trees, the stag was also associated with seasonal changes. Among Celts one of the most popular gods was Cernunnos, the horned one, who was depicted in human form with antlers on his head and a Celtic torc (bracelet) on each arm. Taking into account the stag's attributes, it is interesting to note that Patrick, in order to save himself and his men, changes them all into deer. In the story of David the stag represents the child's future greatness and his conquest of good over evil.

Wolf: A sacred totem of many clans in Europe during early medieval times, the wolf symbolized the virtues of bravery and strength as well as the principle of evil (a werewolf). Wolves figure prominently in the biographies of pagan heroes, including the reputed founders of Rome, Remus and Romulus, who were said to have been suckled by a she-wolf. Because wolves burrow in the earth, Native Americans associate them with secret wisdom and spiritual power. The stories of Maedoc of Ferns are filled with references to wolves.

Bread

Bread, a symbol of transformation and of unity, is produced by a process in which the original ingredients are changed significantly through baking, that is, being near the heat of a fire, another agent of transformation. The Jewish people believed that sharing a meal gave spiritual life to the participants and was a sign of their common unity. Jesus followed in that tradition, making the eucharist *the* act in which his followers would remember him while reminding themselves of their own brother and sisterhood. That ritual, originally celebrated in the homes of the early Christians, eventually was defined in belief and practice as one of the major sacraments of reconciliation of the church. There are many references to the sharing of bread and of eucharist in the hagiographies of the Celtic saints, including the story of Brendan and his fellow pilgrims celebrating eucharist at certain sites each year, and another concerning Ciaran's fabulous bread which, like the eucharist, had the ability to heal every sick person who ate of it.

Fire

Fire is one of the most common symbols in the history of Judeo-Christian spirituality. It represents the power and presence of God. Images of fire, along with those of light, appear repeatedly in the writings of Christian wisdom figures from both the West and East. In the scriptures God speaks to Moses through a burning bush on Mount Sinai and tongues of fire are present at Pentecost; in the fourth century the Egyptian desert mother Amma Syncletica describes God as a consuming fire, and John Cassian associates fire with the highest form of contemplative prayer; in the twelfth century Rhineland mystic Hildegard of Bingen relates how tongues of fire were with her during her spiritual awakening at midlife; and in the fourteenth century, English mystic Richard Rolle describes Jesus as a "honeyed flame." References to fire appear frequently in the stories of the Celtic saints. It is seen by neighbors at the house where Brigit sleeps as a child; it surrounds the room of Ita; and it ascends from the mouth of the holy virgin Samthann to the roof of her home. Bishop Erc sees Brendan's birthplace ablaze, and Ciaran is called "a lamp, blazing with the light of wisdom." Canair sees towers of fire rising from the churches of Ireland; Kevin carries fiery coals; Patrick lights the sacred fires at Tara and his guardian angel speaks to him in a burning bush. All of these images and symbols are used by the hagiographers to say that these people were especially touched by God and manifestations of God's love.

Hair

To many primitive peoples and by all sorts of religious traditions hair represents sexual energy, fertility, creativity, and vital strengths. Hair on one's head was a symbol of spiritual forces, intuitions, insights, spirituality, soul power. Different colors of hair had specific connotations: brown or black hair symbolized dark, terrestrial energy, while golden hair was related to the sun's rays and represented intimacy with God. The length of one's hair and how it was worn also had significance. Samson's story (Jdg 16) tells how the hero was shorn of his strength and freedom when his hair was cut. In the early medieval church, as the priesthood evolved, two styles of tonsure came to symbolize two different ecclesial traditions. The "Petrine" style, in which a round spot toward the back of the head was shaved, was a visible sign of dedication to Rome. The "Celtic" style, probably a carry-over from the pagan druids, in which the whole of the front of the head from ear to ear was shaved while the hair behind was allowed to grow long, represented devotion to Celtic spiritual traditions. Because of the symbolic importance of hair, these two different styles of tonsure became one of the major controversies dividing Roman and Celtic factions at the Synod of Whitby in 664—as we shall see when we consider Hild's stories. There are other references to hair that appear in the saints' Lives: Findbarr has fine hair, symbolizing his closeness to God, and is tonsured early in his life, signifying his vocation to the priesthood; and, in the story of Ethne and Fedelm, the druid Caplit is converted and his hair cut to show his new loyalty to Christ, St. Patrick, and Rome.

Objects

Certain objects that frequently appear in the hagiographies of the Celtic saints are especially equated with spiritual and therefore miraculous powers: a saint's bell, vestments, il-luminated gospels (which remain dry in a rainstorm or when thrown into water!), crozier (a symbol of episcopal powers), or the stone or rock on which the saint or an angel left imprints from hands, head, or feet. These were venerated by later generations as relics. To show the origins of these relics, which were on display at the monasteries where pilgrims came, hagiographers included them in their accounts of the saints.

When these relics (such as books or bells) or other objects (such as land or corn) are exchanged between the saints or given to each other's monasteries, they symbolize the love and mutuality between soul friends, their equality and spiritual kin-ship. There are numerous references to this practice in the follow-ing stories. The story of Brigit giving her father's sword away to a leper, however, has its own significance. In Celtic warrior society the sword was a symbol of potency and virility; for Brigit to give it away symbolized that the source of her spiritual power was not in aggressiveness and intimidation but in mercy and compassion.

Oil

Oil has long been a symbol of healing, of inner strength, and of a life specially consecrated to God. The use of special oils for liturgical functions such as the consecration of kings and priests

---

is a common occurrence in the Hebrew scriptures. The practice was taken over by the early church and eventually used in the celebrations of baptism, confirmation, and holy orders, as well as the consecration of churches and altars. In the hagiographies of the Celtic saints oil is associated with certain saints. References to oil are found particularly in Findbarr's stories, including a vivid account of how oil flowed abundantly at Cork where Findbarr built his church. This indicates that the church and Findbarr himself were sources of healing and spiritual strength.

Trees

Another common symbol, a tree denotes fertility, immortality, and wisdom; it can also connote a person's roots and spiritual heritage. Mircea Eliade, a scholar of world religions, says a tree symbolizes absolute reality, the center out of which all life flows, the life of the cosmos. The Jewish scriptures begin with the account of trees growing in the Garden of Eden: a "Tree of Life" and a "Tree of the Knowledge of Good and Evil" (Gn 2:9). In the Book of Revelation, the last book of the Christian scriptures, "trees of life" are pictured near "the river of life" in the heavenly Jerusalem (Rv 22:2).

Certain trees such as the beech and holly were revered by the pagan Celts. The oak tree symbolized wisdom, and the holly death and regeneration. Their spiritual leaders, the druids and druidesses, are said to have conducted their worship services and taught their students among sacred groves of oaks. A Celtic goddess of the grove, Nemetona, was worshipped at Bath in Britain and in Gaul. Tribal names also indicate close kinship between Celtic people and trees. In the stories of the saints, Samthann encounters a huge oak tree, which she tames with her crozier, and, as we have seen, Ciaran and Enda share a vision of a tree growing in the center of Ireland. This is similar to the vision Native American shaman Black Elk had as a child (and, like Julian of Norwich, while he was ill), and which he believed contained regenerative powers for his tribe. Annie Dillard's description in *Pilgrim at Tinker Creek* of "the tree with the lights in it" came to symbolize her own illumination and spiritual awakening. Among Christians, the Tree of Life found in Genesis becomes the cross on which Christ died, a symbol of God's love and of the way suffering can lead to reconciliation and the birth of compassion, a new way of relating to others and to oneself.

Water

Among many peoples and religious traditions water is a symbol of healing, cleansing, rebirth, and transformation. Because it can reflect light, it also is equated with luminosity and illumination. Water appears in the opening lines of the Book of Genesis and its account of creation; it is associated with Jesus' baptism and the beginning of his public ministry. In all its forms, from sacred springs to holy wells, water was venerated in the Celtic world. The pagan Celts believed that such places were the haunts of female deities. They could obtain special favors, they thought, by throwing offerings into the watery depths. Immersing oneself brought special stamina as well as control over anger and lust. The Celtic saints, as their stories show, are often found praying at night in lakes or oceans. Specific references to the regenerative powers of water appear in the story of a spring gushing forth at David's baptism; in the account of how a dead queen was raised to life by the water Findbarr had blessed; and in the portrayal of the dying Ita blessing water to heal Abbot Aengus. Christians through the ages have seen water as a special symbol of their own baptismal regeneration and rebirth through Christ.

Special Numbers

Besides the presence of these symbols in many of the stories of the Celtic saints, certain numbers had a meaning of their own. For ancient and medieval people, including Greeks, Romans, Jews, Gnostics, Kabbalists, and Celts (both pagan and Christian), certain numbers had special importance, because they believed that everything in this world was a reflection of a greater reality. Numbers, for them, expressed a divine order of things, invisible spiritual forces at work in the universe, a way of expressing and comprehending the meaning of existence. As such, numbers had mystical significance and were equated with spiritual power. Celtic hagiographers knew the symbolic value of these numbers. They used them in their texts to make theological points about the saints, and to increase the reputation and enhance the interest of their own storytelling. Each number had a particular character and meaning of its own. The numbers that appear most frequently in the stories of the Celtic saints are these:

Three: Three was the favorite number of Celtic folklore and hagiography. It was considered a powerful symbol of spiritual strength and intimacy with God, and it represented spiritual synthesis, the reconciliation of apparent opposites. Triads had a remarkable fascination for the Celts, and both pagan and Christian Celts associated them with their deities. The pagans expressed their belief that certain goddesses existed in groups of threes by representing them artistically in such reliefs as those of the "Three Mothers," which appear in practically all parts of the Celtic world. The use of threes was also manifest in the *tricephalos* (three-faced head) found on numerous vases or stones. Christian Celts also symbolized their understanding of divinity with such symbols as the triangle or, as we find in legends about St. Patrick, the shamrock. In the stories of the Celtic saints there are literally hundreds of references to three—from the three angels who appear at Brigit's baptism to the three gifts God gives to Columcille; from the three clerics who foster Findbarr to the three precious stones that appear in Ita's dreams. Even the greatest Celtic religious heroes, Patrick, Brigit, and Columcille, are referred to in common parlance today as "the holy trinity of Irish saints."

Four: The number four symbolized wholeness and harmonious completion. The medieval mind associated the number four with the earth, the four directions of the world, and the seasons. Celts subdivided their land into four quarters, and according to the lawbooks in northern Wales, there were four acres in a homestead. On the Isle of Man four quarterlands at one time formed a *treen*, the smallest unit for administrative purposes. References to the number four appear in the stories of Ciaran with his four sacks of consecrated wheat, of Brigit who cures four sick persons at a certain church, and of Ita who requests four acres of land on which to live.

Five: Another symbol of wholeness, the number five appears in a large number of secular and religious texts. In the Middle Ages it was primarily associated with the Virgin Mary and was generally seen as the number signifying true faith. Medieval Ireland had five great roads and five celebrated hostels; in its literature mythical persons wear fivefold cloaks, and the greatest Irish hero, Cu Chulainn, has five wheels carved on his shield, which in the ancient world represented the cosmos. In the stories of the saints Hild has five students who become bishops, Brendan is fostered by Ita for five years, and Patrick has five companions with him at Tara when he confronts the pagan king.

Seven: A mystical number of special importance for ancient peoples, including Greeks, Romans, Jews, and Celts, the number seven symbolized perfection, perfect order, a complete period or cycle, harmony. Seven is as popular as the number nine in some branches of Celtic literature and of course appears in the saints' stories: Brendan sails for seven years before he reaches the elusive Land of Promise; Cuthbert's spiritual mentor, Boisil, dies on the seventh day; Hild endures a painful illness for seven years; an angel comes to Patrick on the seventh day of each week; Kevin lives for seven years in the wilderness.

Nine: Another prominent mystical number in Celtic tradition, important in divinations and folk cures, nine symbolized great spiritual power, health, fulfillment. Dante was later to equate the number nine with Beatrice, whom he loved dearly and who acts as his guide to heaven in his *Divine Comedy*. In Irish literature there are repeated allusions to companies of nine, which consist of a leader with eight followers, and to houses comprising nine rooms. In Wales there also was a tradition that a complete house should consist of nine component parts. An early Welsh poem mentions the breath of nine maidens, which kindles a certain magical fountain, while in an Irish tale the hero Ruad swims to a secret place and finds nine fair women with whom he sleeps for nine nights under the sea on nine beds of bronze. Nine was evidently a significant unit of time for the Celts, for some scholars assert that they had a nine-day week, or rather a nine-night week (since they reckoned by nights, not days). In the stories of the saints the number nine or its variant appears quite often: Kevin dies at the age of 129, nine heavenly orders of angels are mentioned in the account of Findbarr's death, Non naturally prepares for the birth of David at the end of her ninth month of pregnancy, and a famous Irish high-king is called Niall of the Nine Hostages.

Twelve: An ancient symbol signifying wholeness or completeness, the number twelve has special meaning and is found in many spiritual traditions. In Greek mythology, Odysseus has twelve companions; in the Jewish scriptures there are twelve tribes of Israel; in the Christian gospels twelve apostles accompany Jesus; and in later medieval legends King Arthur has twelve knights of the Round Table. Today we celebrate twelve months of the year. The Celtic hagiographers respected this number's spiritual significance by using it often in their portrayal of the saints: Aidan lives twelve days after the death of the king he loved; Finnian educates the "Twelve Apostles of Ireland"; Findbarr builds twelve churches and is accompanied to Rome by twelve monks; David founds twelve monasteries. Kevin's hagiographer, evidently in order to outdo Brigit's, has twelve angels at Kevin's baptism rather than only three!

We need not be surprised by the symbols and sacred numbers found in the early stories and sayings of the saints. Throughout human history symbolic language has been used not only to describe mysterious events in the outer world, which can be perceived by the human eye (if not always understood!), but also to disclose inner realities: visionary experiences, feelings, intuitions, dreams. These inner experiences, of course, are no less real than the outer ones, for they often determine and profoundly influence the shape and course of outer events as well as the development of character—the distinctive qualities or traits emerging from our deeper selves, what the ancients called, quite simply, our souls. Primitive peoples, including the writers of the gospels, the fathers and mothers of the early church, and the Christian Celts, did not invent the great mysteries described in the saints' lives—birth, love, suffering, forgiveness, death, and rebirth. They experienced them first. If we can identify with them at that level of awareness, we can begin to see that the stories of the Celtic saints, female and male, are really stories about ourselves. They are about our own ability (with the help of God and others, of course) to transcend human pain and suffering, and in the process experience various forms of transformation. Sometimes we undergo such a profound change of heart that it seems we will never be the same again!

Listening With the Heart

By now it should be clear that we should approach the stories and sayings in this book with less of a critical eye to whether the events are historically accurate or verifiable, but rather, as earlier generations did, with an openness to what the stories themselves can teach us about God, holiness, and our own great mysteries.

42

Such an approach presumes some understanding of the early Celtic church's history and spirituality, as well as the significance of the symbols and sacred numbers that appear in hagiographies. It also presupposes that while the stories of the saints contain explicit messages about Christian spirituality and what it means to be fully human today, there is more to these texts than the eye can see or the mind take in. To grasp fully and begin to integrate their spiritual wisdom, we must bring a willingness to reflect quietly upon them and to discern unhurriedly their sometimes hidden meaning. Thus we need to bring to these stories and sayings a compassionate, attentive, listening heart.

By quietly listening to the description of the stages, transitions, and miraculous deeds of a saint's life, we can begin to discern and appreciate our life patterns as well as our own kinship with Jesus. We also might start to recall the happenings (sometimes wondrous?!) told about our birth and early years, and to remember gratefully our significant mentors and how they touched our lives. As we read the stories we might consider what sort of leadership we are presently offering others and what gifts of ours might make a great difference ("miraculous"?) in their lives. In our prayerful reflection we might identify what sorts of trials and tribulations we have encountered and what we have learned in our own "school of suffering." We might ask ourselves what journeys we have already bravely embarked upon—and, if we are to be true to ourselves, what new explorations we may yet have to undertake. We might also, in our quieter moments of listening to the heart, acknowledge with love those special people who have died and the legacy they have passed on to us about the sacredness of life and awesomeness of dying.

By bringing both heart and mind to the stories found in this book—and to our own life experiences—we will truly discover and make our own the wisdom of the Celtic saints, a wisdom that is much more than a mere accumulation of historical knowledge and facts. It is, rather, a way of life, a spirituality lived gratefully each day, one day at a time.

Let us turn now to those early Celtic soul friends, allowing them to become guides to the spiritual heritage which is ours and to the best which lies within us. As friends and mentors of our souls may they help us become more conscious and appreciative of the ancient spiritual traditions in which we stand, so that we might begin to pray not only with our lips and our intellects, but out of the very roots of our lives. Most of all, may they show us wisdom, a Christian wisdom that continues to flourish, like Ciaran's tree growing in the middle of Ireland, capable of teaching all sorts of people, including those of us who live far across the Irish Sea.

They saw a great fruitful tree beside a stream in the middle of Ireland

Stories and sayings from celtic lives

holy island

AIDAN
OF LINDISFARNE

*a*idan was the first bishop and abbot of Lindisfarne, the small island off the coast of northern England located between present-day Berwick-on-Tweed and Bamburgh. A native of Ireland, he was born in the latter part of the sixth century and became a monk of Iona, where St. Columcille had established his monastery earlier. When King Oswald of Northumbria requested a bishop to help convert his pagan subjects, Aidan was consecrated and arrived in Northumbria in 635. He made his headquarters on Lindisfarne. From there he evangelized and founded missionary outposts, including a monastery at Melrose. Among his many Anglo-Saxon protégés were Hild of Whitby and Cuthbert.

His biographer, the Venerable Bede, wrote more affectionately of Aiden than possibly any other saint—except Cuthbert. The qualities that appealed to Bede were the very ones that contributed to Aiden's appeal as a teacher: passionate love of goodness tempered with humility, warmth, and gentleness.

Stories of Aidan also clearly reflect one of the most ancient and enduring traits of authentic Christian spirituality: concern for and love of the poor and strangers. Scholar Dom Gougaud calls Aidan the "true apostle of England," for it was Aidan's missionary outreach in Northumbria that had such a lasting effect upon the conversion of the Saxons. The statue of Aidan which stands on Lindisfarne today, near the medieval abbey ruins, shows him holding the torch of faith he brought to that part of England. Aidan died in 651. His feast day is celebrated August 31.

Aidan's Move to Lindisfarne

As soon as Oswald had come to the throne, he was determined that the whole race under his rule should be filled with the grace of the Christian faith. He therefore sent a special request to the Irish elders, from whom he and his men had received the sacrament of baptism when he was in exile, asking that they send a bishop by whose teaching and ministry the English race over whom Oswald ruled might learn the privileges of faith and receive the sacraments. Oswald's request was immediately granted. The elders sent him Bishop Aidan, a man of outstanding gentleness, devotion, and moderation, who was passionate about God.

When the bishop arrived, the king gave him, according to his wishes, a place for his episcopal see on the island of Lindisfarne. As the tide ebbs and flows, this place is twice daily surrounded by the waves of the sea like an island and twice, when the shore is dry, attached to the mainland once again.

The king humbly and gladly listened to the bishop's advice in all matters, conscientiously seeking to build up and extend the church of Christ in his kingdom. Truly, it was a beautiful sight when the bishop was preaching the gospel to see the king acting as interpreter of the heavenly word for his men, for Aidan was not completely familiar with the English language, while the king had learned Irish perfectly during his long exile.

The Grace of Discretion

There is a story that when King Oswald asked the Irish for a bishop to minister to him and his people, another man of a more rigid disposition was sent first. This man preached to the English for some time unsuccessfully. When he realized that the people were unwilling to listen to him, he returned to his native land. At a meeting he told the elders that he had made no progress instructing the people to whom he had been sent, because they were intractable, stubborn, and barbaric. A long discussion followed as to what ought to be done, for the elders were anxious to give that people the help it asked for. They regretted that the preacher they had sent had not been accepted.

Then Aidan, who was present at the conference, said to the priest: "It seems to me, brother, that you have been unreasonably harsh concerning your ignorant hearers. You did not first offer them the milk of simpler teaching, as the apostle recommends, so that gradually, as they grew strong on the food of God's word, they were capable of receiving more elaborate instruction and of carrying out the higher commandment of God." All eyes were turned on Aidan when they heard these words and everyone present carefully considered what he had said. They then agreed that Aidan was worthy to be made a bishop and that he was the man to send to instruct those unbelievers, for he had proved himself to be preeminently endowed with the grace of discretion, the mother of all virtues. So Aidan was consecrated and sent to preach to the English. As time passed he proved himself to be outstanding not only for moderation and good sense, which the elders had first observed in him, but for many other virtues as well.

Aidan Teaches by Example

Aidan taught the clergy many lessons about the conduct of their lives. Above all he gave them a most beneficial example of abstinence and self-control. The best thing about his teaching to everyone was that he taught no other way of life than that which he himself practiced among his colleagues. Aidan neither sought after nor cared for worldly possessions. Rather, he was happy to hand over to any poor person he met the gifts he had received from kings or the rich of the world. He used to travel everywhere he went, in town and rural areas, not on horseback but on foot, unless he was forced to do otherwise because of some urgent necessity. He did this so that, whenever he saw people whether rich or poor, he might approach them at once. If they were unbelievers, he could strengthen them in the faith, encouraging them by word and deed to practice almsgiving and good works.

Aidan's life was in great contrast to our modern laziness. All who accompanied him, whether they were ordained or laity, had to engage in some form of study; that is, they had to occupy themselves with reading the scriptures or learning the psalms. If it happened, as it rarely did, that Aidan was summoned to feast with the king, he went with one or two of his clergy. After eating a little food, he hurried away either to read with his people or to pray. Neither respect nor fear forced him to remain silent about the sins of the rich, whom he would correct with a stern rebuke when necessary. Aidan never gave money to powerful men of the world, but only food on those occasions when he entertained them. He distributed gifts of money he received from the rich either for the use of the poor, as we have said, or for the redemption of those who had been sold into slavery unjustly.

A Gift-Horse Returned, and a Spiritual Friendship

Another king, King Oswin, gave Aidan an excellent horse so that, though the bishop normally walked, he could ride if he had to cross a river or if he had urgent business. A short time later Aidan was met by a beggar who asked for alms. Aidan dismounted from his horse immediately and offered it to the beggar, for he was extremely compassionate, a friend of the poor, and a real father to the unfortunate. The king was told of this and, when he met the bishop as they were going to dinner, he said, "My lord bishop, why did you give a beggar the royal horse intended for you? Do we not have many less valuable horses or other things which would have been good enough to give to the poor without allowing the beggar to have the horse which I had specially chosen for your own use?" The bishop replied at once, "King, what are you saying? Surely this son of a mare is not dearer to you than that son of God?" After these words were exchanged between them, they went in to dine.

The bishop sat down in his own place and the king, having just come in from hunting, stood with his men warming himself by the fire. Suddenly he remembered the bishop's words. He at once took off his sword, gave it to a retainer, and then running to where the bishop sat, threw himself at his feet and asked his forgiveness. "From now on," he said, "I will never speak of this again. I will not form any opinion as to what wealth of mine or how much of it you should give to the people of God." When the bishop saw this he was greatly alarmed. He got up immediately, raised the king to his feet, and declared that he would be perfectly satisfied if only the king would forget his sorrow and sit down to the feast.

The king, moved by the bishop's requests and commands, recovered his spirit. The bishop, on the other hand, grew sadder and sadder and at last broke into tears. A priest then asked Aidan in his native tongue (which neither the king nor his men understood) why he was weeping. The bishop answered, "I know that the king will not live long, for I never before saw such a humble king. Therefore, I think that he will soon be taken from this life, for this nation does not deserve to have such a ruler." Not much later the bishop's gloomy forebodings were fulfilled. Bishop Aidan himself only lived for twelve days after the murder of the king whom he loved.

Aidan's Tears of Compassion

Another memorable miracle is told about Aidan by those who were in a position to know. During the time of his episcopate a hostile Mercian army under the leadership of Penda had been cruelly devastating the entire kingdom of Northumbria. After Penda had reached the royal city named after a former queen Bebbe [Bamburgh], he could not capture it by assault or siege, so he attempted to set it on fire. He pulled down all the fortifications in the neighborhood of the town and brought there a vast supply of beams, rafters, walls of wattles, and thatched roofs. He then built them up to an immense height around that side of the city facing him.

At that time Bishop Aidan was staying on Farne Island, less than two miles from the city. He often retired there to pray in solitude and silence; in fact, the site of his solitary cell can still be seen on the island. When Aidan saw the tongues of flame and the smoke being carried by the winds above the city walls, he raised his eyes and hands toward heaven and said tearfully, "O Lord, see how much evil Penda is doing!" As soon as he had uttered those words, the winds turned away from the city and carried the flames in the direction of those who had lit them. As a result, some of those men were hurt, while all of them were so terrified that they stopped making any further attempts on the city, realizing that it was divinely protected.

Aidan's Death and Burial

At the time when death came to Aidan he was on a royal estate, not far away from the city of which we have been speaking. Here he had a church and a cell where he frequently stayed while travelling about in the neighborhood to preach. He did the same at the other royal estates, for he had no possessions of his own except the church and a small piece of land around it. His followers erected a tent for him during his illness at the west end of the church, with the tent itself attached to the church wall.

So it happened that Aidan breathed his last while leaning against the buttress which supported the church on the outside. He died August 31, in the seventeenth year of his episcopate. Shortly afterward his body was transferred to the island of Lindisfarne and buried in the cemetery of the brothers. Some time later, when a larger church had been built there and dedicated in honor of the most blessed chief of the apostles, Aidan's bones were transported to it and buried on the right side of the altar, with the honor due to so great a bishop.

BRENDAN
OF CLONFERT

Probably the most widely known Celtic saint, after Patrick and perhaps Brigit, is Brendan the Navigator. Though his life is associated with fabulous legends, it is certain that he was a real person who lived from 486 to 578. Born on the west coast of Ireland, he had St. Ita as his foster-mother for five years. Another important mentor, Bishop Erc, not only baptized Brendan as an infant but ordained him when he had reached manhood.

Brendan began his travels shortly after becoming a priest, and although we have no absolute proof of the places he eventually visited, scholar James Kenney believes that Brendan made a voyage to the Scottish isles and perhaps to the Strathclyde, Cumbria, or Wales. Brendan's main center of activity was probably western Ireland where several places and landmarks are named after him, including Mount Brandon on the Dingle Peninsula. The monastery at Clonfert, founded about 559, is the most important establishment linked with Brendan. At its site today one can see a magnificent ninth- or tenth-century Irish Romanesque doorway, which contains many stone heads of the saints.

The personality of St. Brendan which emerges from the following stories is that of an adventurer willing to take risks. He only does so, however, after consulting with his fellow-monks—certainly a sign of his collaborative nature and his willingness to include others in any major decision that had to be made. Brendan is said to have died at the home of his sister and to be buried at Clonfert. The widespread cult that developed after Brendan's death owed much to the famous *Voyage of Brendan*, a romance of the tenth or eleventh century. It became one of the most popular stories of the Middle Ages. Brendan's feast day is May 16.

The Amazing Birth of Brendan

Brendan was born in the time of Oengus, son of the king of Munster. His noble, devout, and faithful father was Findlug, who lived with his wife in lawful wedlock under the rule of Bishop Erc. Now the mother of Brendan saw a vision before he was born in which it seemed that her bosom was full of pure gold and that her breasts shone like snow. When she told Bishop Erc of this vision, he said that she would give birth to a wondrous child who would be filled with the grace of the Holy Spirit.

On the night of Brendan's birth thirty cows bore thirty calves to Airdi, a very wealthy man who lived some distance away. He went looking for the house in which the little child was born, and when he found it, prostrated himself devoutly before the child and offered him the thirty milk cows and thirty calves. These were the first alms Brendan received. Then the landowner took the child in his arms and said, "He shall be my fosterling forever."

The same night Bishop Erc saw Brendan's birthplace all in one great blaze as was never seen before and a great gathering of angels in shining white garments all around that land. Then Bishop Erc rose early the next morning, went to the house of Findlug, and took the child in his arms, saying: "O man of God and destined servant of God, accept me as your own monk; though many are joyful at your birth, my heart and my soul are even more joyful."

Mobi was the original name given the child by his parents, but when a fair drop fell upon him from heaven, they changed his name to Braenfiend ("fair drop") or Brendan. He was called fair because he was all fair of body and soul.

The Rule of the Irish Saints and Brendan's Desire to Travel

After learning the canon of the Old and New Testaments, Brendan wished to write out and learn the rule of the saints of Erin. Bishop Erc gave him permission to go and learn this rule, for he knew it was from God that this desire had come to him. He said to Brendan, "Come back to me, and bring the rules with you, that I may ordain you when you return."

Brendan went to consult his foster-mother, Ita, who also encouraged him to learn the rule of the saints of Ireland. So then, after writing the rules of the saints, their customs, and their devotions, Brendan returned to Bishop Erc and was ordained.

It was after this that a great love for the Lord grew in his heart, and he yearned to leave his country, his parents, and the inheritance of his ancestors. Brendan begged the Lord to give him some unknown country to visit, far removed from humankind.

Barinthus's Tale of a Mysterious Island

A certain holy man came to Brendan. His name was Barinthus, and he was King Niall's grandson. As Brendan was asking him many questions, the man prostrated himself on the ground mourning and weeping. Brendan raised him to his feet, kissed him, and said, "It is better to rejoice than to mourn, and by God's passion I command you to speak of God and satisfy our souls."

After some further conversation between them, the holy man began to tell Brendan of a certain island: "I had a son named Mernoc who fled from me because he did not wish to remain in the same place with me. He found an island near a certain mountain, and sometime later, when I heard that he had many monks with him and that many miracles were manifested through him, I went to visit him. When I had been traveling for three days, my son came to meet me with the brothers of his community, for God had revealed my coming to him.

"My son and I traversed the island, and after we had gone over it, he took me with him to the shore where there was a boat. Then he said to me: 'Dear father, get into the boat so that we may go and see the island that is called The Land of the Saints, which God will promise to those who come after us.' When we had entered the boat, a mist fell upon us, so that we could hardly see the prow of the ship. About an hour later a great light came upon us, and we saw a beautiful island, full of fragrant blossoms and apples. Every herb or tree on the island was laden with fruit. We landed, and for fifteen days we walked the island without finding any end to it. The stones of the island were all jewels.

"Oh, Brendan," said Barinthus, "I remained a fortnight in that place with my son, without eating or drinking. At the end of forty days I returned to my own brethren and my own cell."

When Brendan and his followers heard this, they bowed their heads to the ground, praised God greatly, and said, "Blessed is God in his own gifts, and holy in all his works, because he has revealed so many miracles to his servants, and has fed us this day until we are filled with spiritual food."

Brendan's Decision-Making and Setting Sail

When Barinthus had departed, Brendan collected fourteen monks from his community and went with them to a secluded spot. There he told them: "Beloved brothers, I am asking your advice and help, for my heart and thoughts are fixed on one single desire, if it be God's desire, and that is to seek the land of which Barinthus told us, the land God has promised to those who come after us. What do you think?"

They all said with one voice: "Beloved father, whatever you wish is our desire. We are ready to face death or life together with you. There is but one other thing to do. Let us seek to discern the will of God, and to fulfill it."

So Brendan with his family decided to fast for forty days and nights, so that God would help them, and guide them.

Brendan slept after this, and heard the voice of an angel from heaven saying, "Arise, Brendan, for what you have requested from God, you shall receive; you will visit the Land of Promise at last."

Brendan arose, and his heart rejoiced at the answer of the angel. He went by himself to a solitary place. Scanning the ocean on every side, he saw a wondrous and fair island with angels hovering about it. Brendan remained in that place some time and slept once again. Again the angel of God came to converse with him, and said, "From now on, I will be with you, and I will show you one day the fair island which you have seen, and which you hope to visit." Brendan wept tears of joy at the angel's words and gave thanks to God.

Then Brendan set forth with fourteen companions, travelling westward. The wind carried them to the port of Aran. Brendan said farewell to Enda and the other saints of Aran and left a blessing with them. Then they sailed due west across the ocean. It was summer, and they had a favorable brisk wind behind them, so they did not have to row. After they had spent ten days in this way, the wind lowered its loud voice and whistling. With its force spent, they were compelled to take up the oars. Brendan spoke to them, saying: "Do not be afraid, for we have our God as our guide and helper. Put up your oars, and do not toil anymore; God will guide this boat and company as God pleases."

A Liturgical Cycle Repeated Each Year

After many adventures, the company saw an island in the distance. Brendan said, "Over there is the island on which we were last year on the day of the Lord's Supper." When they had landed, the holy man whom they had previously met on this island came to them with great joy, kissed their feet, and began loudly to praise the Lord. He speedily prepared a bath for them, clothed them all in new garments, and they celebrated the Lord's Passion until Easter Eve. When they had celebrated the service for Saturday, the man said to Brendan: "Embark, and celebrate Easter as you did last year. And from Easter on, go to the Paradise of Birds, and take what you need in food and drink. I will pay you a visit on the second Sunday that is coming." The monks departed as the holy man had recommended and celebrated Easter on the island where they had been the previous year.

From there they went to the Paradise of Birds where they stayed until the octave of Pentecost. The holy man came to them as he had promised and brought with him all the things they needed. They greeted one another joyfully, as they had done before.

At the moment they sat down to eat, a bird alighted on the prow of the ship and made music as sweet as an organ with its wings, beating them on the sides of the boat. Then Brendan perceived that it was telling them something, and he listened as the bird spoke: "On this journey four seasons have been determined for you; that is, the day of the Lord's Supper is to be celebrated with the holy man, Easter on the island, which is really the back of a sea monster, and from Easter to Pentecost with us on Paradise Island, and Christmas on the Island of Ailbe up to Mary's feast of Candlemas. At the end of the seventh year you will reach the land you are seeking, and you will be there forty days and then borne back to your homeland." On hearing this Brendan lay on the ground, wept, and gave praise and thanks to God, the Creator of all things. The bird returned to its own place, the holy man departed leaving his blessing with them, and Brendan and his

61

men stayed until the time had come for them to leave as well. Then they set out upon the ocean.

Brendan's Return and Ita's Advice

Now when Brendan had been on this voyage five years, following the cycle of feast days that had been prescribed, he returned to his own country. The people of his land and tribe came to meet him, and asked what things he had brought back on his boats. Some gave gifts and treasures to him, and many of them decided to follow Christ. Brendan performed many mighty miracles there. Sick folk were healed, prisoners set free, demons and vices expelled. He then spoke with his foster-father, Bishop Erc, and next went to the place where his foster-mother, Ita, lived. He asked her what he should do with reference to his voyaging. Ita welcomed him as she would have welcomed Christ and his apostles and said to him: "Ah, dearly beloved son, why did you go on your journey without seeking advice from me first? For the country you are seeking from God you will never find on these soft, dead skins, for it is a holy consecrated land and no human blood was ever shed on it. Build boats made of timber, and you will find the land that you are searching for." So Brendan went into the Connacht region and built an excellent and very large boat. He then embarked with his company and people. They took with them various herbs and seeds to store on board, as well as craftsmen and smiths who had begged Brendan to let them go along. Then Brendan and his company went back again over the surface of the sea and the great ocean.

A Second Voyage and the Land of Promise

One day when Brendan and his company were traversing the sea, they finally happened upon the little country they had been seeking for seven years; that is, the Land of Promise. As it says in the proverb, "He who seeks, finds." When they approached the land and were entering its harbor, they heard the voice of a certain elder speaking to them: "O holy pilgrims, tired men who have searched for this country for so long, remain where you are a little while and rest from your labors." When they had done so, the elder said, "Dear brothers in Christ, do you not see that this is glorious and lovely land on which human blood has never been shed? Leave everything that you have in your boat, except the few clothes you are wearing, and come on shore." When they had landed, each of them kissed the others, and the elder wept tears of great joy. "Search and see the borders and regions of Paradise where you will find health without sickness, pleasure without contention, union without quarrel, feasting without diminution, meadows filled with the sweet scent of fair flowers, and the attendance of angels all around. Happy indeed is he whom Brendan, son of Findlug, shall summon here to join him, to inhabit forever and ever the island on which we are now."

When they saw Paradise in the midst of the ocean waves, they marvelled at the wonders of God and his power.

Homecoming at Aran

After this, Brendan and his monks proceeded to their boat and departed from Paradise. Nothing unusual is narrated of their journeying until they came to eastern Aran after two years on this voyage and five on the former voyage. It was thus seven years in all that it took them on the two voyages to reach the Land of Promise. As a poet said:

Seven years in all were they
On the voyage—fair was the band—
Seeking the land of promise
With its flocks, a strong subtle turn.

And they found it at last
In the high meadows of the ocean,
An island rich, everlasting, undivided,
Abounding in salmon, fair and beauteous.

When they reached Aran, they received a great welcome such as Christ and his apostles might receive. They related the story of their many adventures to the people of Aran, from first to last. When Enda and his companions heard the story, they wept exceedingly, possessed as they were with great joy. The people tried to detain Brendan, but he told them, "Here is not my place of resurrection." He and his monks stayed one more month, tired from their rowing. At the end of that time they left Aran and proceeded to Ireland, where they dropped anchor in the sea near Limerick.

Brendan's Visit to Britain, and His and Brigit's Mutual Confession

One day Ita advised Brendan to cross the sea: "A foreign land is calling you, so that you can instruct the souls of those over there. Go now, depart from here." Brendan left immediately for the land of Britain. It was winter when he arrived there, at the place where Gildas the Briton was. Gildas told his people to prepare a great feast for Brendan and his companions. They stayed there for three days and three nights. After Brendan had blessed the monastery of Gildas and the neighboring tribes, they departed. The people and the tribes wept greatly, for they loved Brendan as if he had been their father.

One day Brendan was on a lofty crag on the Isle of Ailec, near Britain, when he saw two sea monsters coming from the depth of the sea and fighting desperately together, trying to drown each other. Then one of the sea monsters tried to fly, and the other pursued it. The flying monster said with a human voice: "I beseech you in the name of St. Brigit to let me be!" The other monster left it immediately and went into the depth of the sea.

Brendan was astonished at this. He returned to his companions, and said to them: "Let us depart quickly for Ireland, so that we can speak with St. Brigit." When he reached the place where Brigit was, he told her of the conversation between the two monsters and asked her, "What is it that you do for God more than I, since monsters call upon your name, though you are absent, rather than mine, though present?"

Brigit said to Brendan: "Make your confession, O cleric, first, and I will afterward." "I declare," said Brendan, "that since I first became a monk, I never crossed seven furrows without turning my mind to God." "Good is your confession," said Brigit. "So now make your confession to me," replied Brendan. "I confess," said Brigit, "that since I first fixed my mind on God, I have never taken it from him, and never will until Doomsday. You, however, so constantly face the dangers of sea and land that you must give your attention to them; it is not because you forget God that your mind is fixed on him only at every seventh furrow."

"It seems to us, O nun," said Brendan, "that the monsters are right to give honor to you."

Brendan and a Young Harpist

After this Brendan and his company returned to Ireland and proceeded until they had reached Clonfert. Brendan was there on Easter Day in the seventh year before his death. The canonical hours had been celebrated in the church, the sermon preached, and Mass said. When midday came the monks went to the refectory, while Brendan was left alone in the church. As they ate, a young cleric who had a little harp in his hand began to play to them. They blessed him for it.

"I would be very happy," he said to them, "if Brendan would allow me to play three strains for him in the church." "He will not let you," said the monks. "For the past seven years Brendan has never smiled, nor listened to any music in the world. Two balls of wax tied together with a thread are always on the book in front of him, and whenever he hears any music, he puts them into his ears." "Still, I will go to play the harp for him," the young cleric replied.

So the young man approached the church with his already tuned harp in his hand. "Please open the door," he said. "Who is there?" asked Brendan. "A young cleric to play the harp for you," said he. "Play outside," said Brendan. "If you do not mind," the cleric replied, "I would be very happy if you would admit me into the church." "Very well, " Brendan said, "open the door." The young cleric set his harp on the floor between his feet. Brendan put the two balls of wax into his ears. "I do not want to play for you," the cleric said, "unless you take out the wax." "I will do as you like," Brendan told him, and put the balls on the book in front of him. Then the cleric played three strains on the harp. "A blessing on you, young man," said Brendan, "and the music of heaven for you hereafter."

Then Brendan put the wax back into his ears, for he did not care to listen to any music of this world. "Why do you not listen to music?" asked the young cleric. "Is it because you consider it so bad?" "No," Brendan replied, "not that, but seven years ago this very day in this church after Mass, all the young clerics had gone to the refectory and I was left here alone. A great yearning for the Lord seized me after communion, and while in that state of fear and trembling, I saw a bird move from the window and settle on the altar. I could not look upon it, for beams of light like the sun

---

65

surrounded it. Then the bird said to me, 'Give me your blessing.' I said, 'May God bless you! But who are you?' 'Michael the angel,' said he. 'I have come to speak with you.' 'I thank God,' said I, 'but why are you here?' 'To play for you, and for the Lord.' 'You are welcome to do so,' said I. Then he drew his beak across his wing, and I listened until the same hour on the following day when he said farewell."

Here Brendan drew his bookmark across the neck of the young cleric's harp and asked, "Does that seem pleasing to you, young man? I declare before God that the sweetest music in the world, compared with that music, is no more than the noise made by this bookmark. But take my blessing, and may heaven be yours in return for playing for me." This place in Clonfert where the young cleric played his harp for Brendan became Brendan's Hermitage.

Brendan's Visit to His Sister, and His Death

After this Brendan went to visit his sister Brig at the fort which is now called Enach Duin. After traversing the great perils of sea and land, after raising dead men, healing lepers, the blind, deaf, and lame, and all kinds of sick folk, after founding many cells, monasteries, and churches, after preeminence in pilgrimage and ascetic devotion, and after performing mighty works and miracles too numerous to mention, Brendan drew near to the day of his death. When Brendan had received the body and blood of Christ at Mass on Sunday, he said: "God is calling me to the eternal kingdom. My body must be taken to Clonfert, for angels will be in attendance there and there is my place of resurrection. Make a small chariot, and let one of you go with it to convey my body. If it were a large wagon with numerous attendants, the tribes would notice it and dispute over my body."

When he had finished, he blessed his sister Brig and all the brethren, and upon reaching the threshold of the church, he said, "In manus tuas, Domine" ("Into your hands, O Lord"). Then, after completing ninety-three years on earth, he sent forth his spirit. The next day Brendan's body was placed on the chariot, as he had said, and a single brother went with him to Clonfert. There his body was buried with great honor and reverence, with psalms and hymns and spiritual songs in honor of the Father, and of the Son, and of the Holy Spirit.

BRIGIT
OF KILDARE

St. Brigit is the most famous female leader of the early Celtic church, a soul friend with whom that ancient tradition of spiritual guidance is very much identified. She lived in Ireland from about 452 to 524, governing both women and men in her double monastery at Kildare. Nuns at her monastery are said to have kept an eternal flame burning there, a custom that may have originated with female druids residing at that spot long before the saint arrived. Their leader supposedly was a high priestess who bore the name of the goddess Brigit or Brighid ("the exalted one"), a deity of wisdom, poetry, fire, and hearth. Like other Celtic goddesses who sometimes appear in groups of threes, the goddess Brigit was associated with two sisters by the same name—one who was patron of healing, and the other of the smith's craft. These attributes were eventually identified with Brigit, the saint, whose feast day, February 1, came to be celebrated on the same day as that of the pagan goddess. Early hagiographers also portray crucial turning points of Brigit's life and ministry as touched with fire. It is clear that St. Brigit stands on the boundary between pagan mythology and Christian spirituality.

Brigit was called "the Mary of the Gael" and considered during the Middle Ages as the patron saint of travellers and pilgrims. In Ireland she is still prayed to as the guardian of farm animals, of healers, and of midwives. Except for a round tower and a restored medieval cathedral, little remains now at Kildare. Even though the holy fires have long been extinguished, the reputation of Brigit as a spiritual guide remains. She is known for many leadership traits: patience, prayerfulness, inclusivity, and most of all, compassion. The latter quality was the basis of her spiritual power and of her ministry as a soul friend.

Brigit, Daughter of a Slave

Brigit was the daughter of Dubthach, son of Demre, son of Bresal. Before she was born, Dubthach bought a slave woman named Broicsech. Dubthach had intercourse with that slave, and she became pregnant by him. Jealousy of the slave seized Dubthach's wife, and she said to Dubthach, "Unless you sell the slave so that she is far from here, I will take my dowry from you and I will leave you." Dubthach, however, did not want to sell the slave.

Dubthach and the slave went in a chariot past the house of a certain druid. When the druid heard the noise of the chariot he went to meet Dubthach and asked whose was the woman with him in the chariot. "Mine," said Dubthach. The druid asked if she was pregnant by anyone. "She is pregnant by me," Dubthach replied. The druid then prophesied: "Marvelous will be the child that is in her womb. No one on earth will be like her." "But my wife wants me to sell this slave," Dubthach sighed. "Never mind," the druid said, "for the offspring of your wife shall serve the offspring of the slave, for this slave will bring forth a wonderful, radiant daughter who will shine like the sun among the stars of heaven." Dubthach was thankful for that answer, for until then no daughter had been born to him.

Born on the Threshold in a Druid's House

Dubthach sold Broicsech to a poet because of his wife's jealousy. On the night that the poet reached his home, a holy man happened to be in the house entreating the Lord and praying. He saw a flame and a fiery pillar rising from the place where Broicsech was living. A certain druid went to the poet's house, and the poet sold the slave to him but did not sell the offspring that lay in her womb. Then the druid took Broicsech home.

When the slave went at sunrise with a vessel full of milk in her hand, she put one of her two feet over the threshold of the house, while leaving the other foot inside. At that moment she brought forth her daughter, Brigit. The maidservants washed Brigit with the milk that was still in her mother's hand.

On a certain day the slave went to milk her cattle, and left the girl alone sleeping in her house. Neighbors saw the house on fire, as if a single flame reached from earth to heaven. When they came to rescue her, the fire disappeared, but they saw it as a sign that the girl was full of the grace of the Holy Spirit.

Then this holy virgin grew to be a young woman, and everything which her hand touched increased. She tended the sheep, she satisfied the birds, she fed the poor. Once when the druid was sleeping, he saw three clerics in shining garments who poured oil on the girl's head and completed the ritual of baptism in the usual manner. Those were really three angels. The third angel told the druid that the name of the girl was *Sancta Brigida*, that is, Saint Brigit. The druid arose and related what he had seen.

She Gives Away Her Father's Sword

Then Brigit went with her mother to her father's house. Whatever her hands would find or would get of her father's wealth and food and property she gave to the poor and needy of the Lord.

A leper came to her one day and asked Brigit to give him something in God's name. She handed down from the chariot her father's sword. When her father returned, he asked Brigit what she had done with his sword. Brigit said, "I gave it to a poor man who came to beg of me." Dubthach was extremely angry with her for having given the sword away and took her to the king to sell her. When Brigit came before the king, he said, "Why did you steal your father's property and wealth, and, what is worse, why have you given the sword away?" Brigit said, "The Virgin Mary's Son knows, if I had your power, with all your wealth, and with all your Leinster, I would give them all to the Lord of the Elements." Said the king to Dubthach: "It is not right for us to deal with this young woman, for her merit before God is higher than ours." Thus was Brigit saved from bondage.

Brigit Is Ordained a Bishop

Brigit and certain virgins went to take the veil from Bishop Mel. He was very happy to see them. Because of her humility, Brigit held back so that she might be the last to whom a veil should be given. A fiery pillar rose from her head to the roof of the church. Bishop Mel said to her: "Come, holy Brigit, that a veil may be placed on your head before the other virgins." Then, it happened that, through the grace of the Holy Spirit, the form of ordaining a bishop was read over Brigit. Mac Caille, Bishop Mel's assistant, said that a bishop's rank should not be conferred on a woman. Bishop Mel replied: "But I do not have any power in this matter. That dignity has been given by God to Brigit, beyond every other woman." Therefore, the people of Ireland from that time to this give episcopal honor to Brigit's successor.

Brigit's Ministry as a Wounded Healer

At another time Brigit was afflicted by a disease of the eyes, and her head seemed exceedingly weary. When Bishop Mel heard of this he said: "Let us go together to seek a physician, that your headaches may be healed." As they were on the road, Brigit fell out of her chariot and hit her head against a stone. She was severely wounded and the blood gushed out. Two women who were lying on the road were healed by that blood. When the leech (physician) saw Brigit's wound, he said: "You should not seek any other physician from this time forward, except the Physician who healed you on this occasion, for, even if all the doctors of Ireland would attend to you, they could do nothing better." In that way Brigit was healed.

Brigit went to a certain church to celebrate Easter. The prioress of the church said to her maidens that on Maundy Thursday one of them should minister to the old men and to the weak and feeble persons who were living in the church. Not one of the women volunteered for that ministry. Brigit, however, said, "Today I will minister to them." There were four sick persons in the church: a consumptive man, a lunatic, a blind man, and a leper. Brigit ministered to these four, and they were healed from their diseases.

Brigit's desire was to satisfy the poor, to expel every hardship, to spare every miserable person. Her heart and her mind were a throne of rest for the Holy Spirit. She was dedicated to God, compassionate toward the wretched, and splendid in miracles and marvels. Thus her name among created things is Dove among birds, Vine among trees, Sun among stars.

She Founds Her Monastic City at Kildare

Brigit went to Bishop Mel so that he might come and mark out her city for her. When they came to the place in which Kildare stands today, Ailill, son of Dunlang, chanced to be coming at the same time with a hundred loads of wood drawn by horses. Brigit's women went to him to ask for some of the wood, but Ailill refused to give them any. Immediately his horses were struck to the ground beneath the wagonloads of wood. Even when stakes and rods were taken from them, they could not rise until Ailill had offered the hundred wagons to Brigit. Brigit's great house in Kildare was then built, and Ailill fed the builders and paid them their wages. So Brigit blessed him and promised that his descendants would inherit the kingship of Leinster until Doomsday.

Anyone Without a Soul Friend

A young cleric of the community of Ferns, a foster-son of Brigit's, used to come to her with wishes. He was often with her in the refectory to partake of food. One time, after coming to communion, she struck a bell. "Well, young cleric there," said Brigit, "do you have a soul friend?"

"I have," replied the young man.

"Let us sing his requiem," said Brigit, "for he has died. I saw when you had eaten half your portion of food that that portion was put in the trunk of your body, but that you were without any head. For your soul friend has died, and anyone without a soul friend is like a body without a head. Eat no more until you get a soul friend."

The Wild Fox and Brigit's Compassion

On another occasion a foolish man saw a fox walking toward the castle of the king, and thought it was a wild animal. Dimwitted as he was, he was ignorant of the fact that the fox was tame, a frequent visitor to the king's court, trained in various skills. It was, in short, a grand and distinguished mascot of the king and his nobles. While a huge crowd watched, the poor fool killed the fox. At once the man was denounced by those who had witnessed the deed, put in irons, and dragged before the king. When the king learned what had happened, he was enraged. He ordered the man to be killed unless a fox, as clever as his own, were given to him in recompense. The king also ordered the man's wife, his children, and all that he had to be reduced to slavery.

When holy and venerable Brigit learned what had happened, she felt great compassion for the miserable fool and ordered her chariot to be prepared. Grieving in her innermost heart for the poor unfortunate who was unjustly condemned, she rode along the road that led to the castle of the king, pouring out prayers to God as she passed over the flat plain. There was no delay, for the Lord heard Brigit as she prayed so fervently. He commanded one of his wild foxes to go to her. When the fox approached the speeding chariot of holy Brigit, it leaped up lightly and landed inside. Then, nestling up under the fold of Brigit's garment, it sat tamely in the chariot with her.

When Brigit arrived at the king's castle, she began to beg that the poor fool who was being held be freed of his bonds. The king was unwilling to listen to her pleas, swearing that he would not free the man unless he were recompensed with a fox as gentle and as clever as his had been. At this point Brigit brought forth her fox into the center of the court. The fox played before the eyes of everyone in exactly the same way as the other fox had done, acting before the king and all those gathered there with the same gestures, cleverness, and docility as the first. When the king saw this, he was satisfied and, acknowledging the resounding approval of the multitude who were in admiration of this wondrous event, he ordered the man released.

Not much later, when Brigit had returned to her home, the same fox, sad and tormented by the crowds, fled quickly through the remote forests and reached its own cave unharmed.

Brigit's Last Days

The Lord performed many miracles and marvels for Brigit, so many that no one could declare them all unless Brigit's own soul or an angel of God should help them.

Now Nindid Pure-hand came from Rome during Brigit's last days, after she had founded many cells and churches and after she had performed miracles and marvels as numerous as the grains of sand on the seashore or the stars in the heavens. He was called Nindid Pure-hand because he never put his hand to his side when Brigit prayed an Our Father with him. After she had received holy communion from him, she sent her spirit to heaven. Her relics remain on earth with great honor and dignity, with many miracles and marvels. Her soul is like a sun in the heavenly kingdom among the choirs of angels and archangels. Although her honor is great here on earth, greater by far will it be when she shall arise like a shining lamp in completeness of body and soul at the great assembly of Doomsday. She will arise in union with cherubim and seraphim, in union with the Son of Mary the Virgin, in the union that is nobler than every union, in the union of the Holy Trinity, Father, Son, and Holy Spirit.

I beseech the mercy of Almighty God, through holy Brigit's intercession, that we may all deserve that unity, may we attain it, may we dwell with it forever!

CANAIR
OF BANTRY BAY

Little is known about this Irish woman solitary, except what appears in a medieval hagiography of St. Senan, a holy monk who lived on Scattery Island, off the western Irish coast. In that account Canair (or Cannera) lived and prayed for many years in a cell she had built near Bantry Bay. Shortly before her death she decided to visit Senan's island home. Considering her words to Senan about his lack of hospitality, she may well have been the first Irish feminist! She also evidently had a positive effect on the older man, for early legends say that Aidan of Lindisfarne was a disciple of Senan, and he certainly, as we have seen, was a significant mentor for both women and men.

Canair died about the year 530. Her feast day is January 28. The site of her partially submerged grave is marked with a simple flag and can still be seen in the waters off Scattery Island. A sixteenth-century poet invoked her as patron of seamen, and Irish sailors throughout the centuries have saluted Canair's grave before setting sail.

Canair's Persistence

Canair the Pious, a holy woman living in the south of Ireland, set up a hermitage in her own territory. One night, while she was praying, all the churches of Ireland appeared to her in a vision. It seemed as if a tower of fire rose up to heaven from each of the churches. The highest of the towers of fire, and the straightest toward heaven, was that which rose from Inis Cathaig (Scattery Island). "Fair is Senan's cell," Canair said. "I will go there, that my resurrection may be near it." She went immediately, without guidance except for the tower of fire, which she saw continuing to blaze day and night until she arrived. Now, when she had reached the shore, she walked upon the sea as if she were on smooth land until she came to Inis Cathaig. Senan knew that she was coming, and he went to the harbor to meet and welcome her.

"Yes, I have come," Canair told him.

"Go to your sister who lives on the island to the east of this one, so that you may be her guest," said Senan.

"That is not why I came," said Canair, "but that I may find hospitality with you on this island."

"Women cannot enter on this island," Senan replied.

"How can you say that?" asked Canair. "Christ is no worse than you. Christ came to redeem women no less than to redeem men. He suffered for the sake of women as much as for the sake of men. Women as well as men can enter the heavenly kingdom. Why, then, should you not allow women to live on this island?"

"You are persistent," said Senan.

"Well then," Canair replied, "will I get what I ask for? Will you give me a place to live on this island and the holy sacrament of eucharist?

"Yes, Canair, a place of resurrection will be given you here on the brink of the waves," said Senan. She came on shore then, received the sacrament from Senan, and immediately went to heaven.

Because of Canair's holiness, God grants that whoever visits her church before going on the sea shall not be drowned.

CIARAN
OF CLONMACNOIS

Ciaran of Clonmacnois lived from about 512 to 545. He was one of the great monastic founders called the "Twelve Apostles of Ireland" educated by Finnian at Clonard. Following in his mentor's footsteps, Ciaran established one of the largest, richest, and most important monastic centers of learning in the entire Celtic church. His father, Boite, was a carpenter, craftsman, and chariot-maker in the midland kingdom of Mide, Meath. When he found the taxes too oppressive, he and his wife crossed over the Shannon to Magh Ai in northern Roscommon where Ciaran was born. There are numerous references in Ciaran's hagiography to his love of learning, which may have been a direct inheritance from his maternal grandfather who was a bard, poet, and historian. Ciaran also seems to have had a great capacity for friendships. He had a broad network of soul friends scattered throughout the early Irish church, including Columcille of Iona (a fellow student), Finnian of Clonard (his tutor), Enda of the Aran Islands (a mentor), Senan of Scattery Island (a colleague), and Kevin of Glendalough (a close friend).

Ciaran founded the monastery of Clonmacnois on the banks of the Shannon River in late 544. Less than a year later, on September 9, 545, he died unexpectedly at the age of thirty-three, perhaps, like his former tutor Finnian, a victim of the yellow plague. Clonmacnois today has some of the finest monastic ruins and high crosses in all of Ireland. It is visited by many tourists and pilgrims each year. Ciaran's feast day is September 9.

Soul Friend and Lamp of Wisdom

Charity is the proper virtue of Christians. Other virtues may belong to both good and evil people, but only a good person has charity. That is why Jesus, the peacemaker of God and the savior of the whole world, said: "This is how all will know that you are my disciples, that you love one another as I have loved you." Now a multitude of sons and daughters of life, from that time to this, have fulfilled the advice Jesus gave them and loved as he loved. Special recognition has been given to the high-priest and apostle holy Ciaran, son of a craftsman, for his tremendous charity.

This Ciaran has been called venerable, a soul friend, a wonderworker, a man whose brilliance in miracles and marvels, virtues and good deeds, lit the Western world. Regarding his heavenly genealogy, he was the son of the Carpenter who made heaven and earth and all that is. According to his earthly genealogy, he was the son of a carpenter who built chariots and practiced other arts besides. For the delight of the souls of the faithful, we set forth a brief record of the miracles and of the marvels of that holy man, who ranked as one of Christ's apostles in this world. Columcille described him as a lamp, blazing with the light of wisdom, whose founding of a lofty church brought wisdom to all the churches of Ireland.

Ciaran's First Tutor and the Tale of a Fox

After Ciaran was born he was baptized by deacon Justus, for it is only right that the righteous should be baptized by a righteous one.

This was the work that his parents gave him to do: to herd cattle in the same way as David, son of Jesse, had herded sheep. For God knew that Ciaran would be a wise leader over a great herd, that is, the herd of the faithful.

Something marvelous happened while he was watching the cattle some distance from the home of his foster-father, deacon Justus, at Fidarta. Even though there was a great distance between them, he was able to hear what his tutor had to say as if they were side by side.

One day a fox came out of the forest and approached Ciaran, and Ciaran treated it gently. It then visited him quite often, until finally Ciaran asked the fox to do him a favor, namely, to carry his psalter back and forth between him and his tutor, deacon Justus. For when it was said at Fidarta, "In the name of the Father, and of the Son, and of the Holy Spirit," Ciaran at one location could hear the entire lesson of his tutor at another until he was done. So the fox used to wait patiently beside Justus until the writing of the lesson on wax had come to an end and then carry it to Ciaran. Once, however, his natural inclinations overcame the fox, and he began to eat the book, for he was greedy about the leather straps that were wrapped around it on the outside. While he was eating the book, Oengus, son of Crimthann, came toward him with a band of men and with greyhounds. They hunted that fox, and he could not find shelter in any place except under Ciaran's cowl. God's name and Ciaran's were magnified not only by the book being saved from the fox, but by the fox being saved from the hounds. That book is today called *Polaire Ciarain* (*Ciaran's Tablets*)

There is a lesson in this, for there are wicked people who live near the church and benefit from it by receiving baptism, communion, food, and instructions. Nevertheless, they do not stop persecuting the church until a king persecutes them, or they face their own mortality, or an unknown illness comes their way. Only then do they seek protection from the church, just as the fox hid under Ciaran's cowl.

Ciaran's Move to Clonard

When it was time for Ciaran to go as a scholar to Finnian of Clonard in order to learn wisdom, he asked his mother and his father for a cow, so that he might take her with him. Ciaran's mother said she would not give him the cow. So he blessed a cow of the herd, who from that time on was called *Odhar Ciarain* (Ciaran's Dun-Cow). She, with her calf, went with Ciaran to Clonard. There he drew a line between them with his staff, for there was no fence to separate them, and the cow was licking the calf. After that, neither of them would come over that line. That cow's milk was divided among Finnian's protégés, the "Twelve Apostles of Ireland," along with their households and with their guests, and it used to be enough for all of them. As the poet said:

Full fifty and a hundred
Ciaran's Dun used to feed,
Both guests, and the poor,
And folk of the refectory and upper room.

Now the Dun's hide is still in Clonmacnois, and whoever dies and is laid on that hide will obtain eternal life.

These were the twelve bishops of Ireland who lived at Finnian's school in Clonard, as a poet said:

Two Finnians, two chaste Columcilles,
Ciaran, Cainnech, fair Comgall,
Two Brendans, Ruadan the handsome one,
Ninnid, Mobi, Nat-fraich's son, that is,
Molaise of Devenish.

This is the rule they had: each bishop on a certain day was to take his turn grinding meal at the mill. But angels used to grind at the mill for Ciaran on the day that was his.

Ciaran's Helpful Stag and His Generosity
to a Fellow-Scholar

At the school of Clonard a stag used to visit Ciaran, and he would put his book on the deer's horns. One day when Ciaran heard the bell, he rose suddenly at its sound, and even more swiftly the stag arose, running away with the book on his horns. Though it rained that day and that night as well, not a single letter in the open book was moistened. The next day, when the cleric arose, the deer came to him with the unharmed book.

To that same school, Ninnid Slant-eye came to study with Finnian, and he had no book. "Ask for a book," Finnian told him. Ninnid made the rounds of the school but could not obtain a book from any of the scholars. "Did you go to the tender youth who is north of the green (an open field)?" asked Finnian. "I will go now," Ninnid said.

When Ninnid arrived at his cell, Ciaran had reached the middle text of Matthew's gospel: *Omnia quaecumque vultis ut faciant homines vobis ita et vos faciatis illis* ("All those things which you want people to do for you, you also must do for them"). "I have come to borrow a book," Ninnid told him. "Mercy on us!" Ciaran replied. "It is for this I read, since the text says to me that I should do to every one what I desire to be done to me. Take this book." His companions asked him the next day where his book was. "He gave it to me," Ninnid announced. One of them in the school then said, "Let Ciaran Half-Matthew be his name." "No," said Finnian, "let us rather call him Ciaran Half-Ireland, for half of Ireland will be his, and ours will be its other half."

Ciaran Sets Limits in a Relationship and Bakes Some Fabulous Bread

After that, the school experienced a time of famine. It became necessary for each of them to protect the sack of grain that was carried to the mill. It happened to be Ciaran's turn to carry a sack of oats to the mill. When opening the sack he said, "O Lord, I should like this to be beautiful wheat, that it would bring great, pleasant, and delightful satisfaction to the elders." So it came to pass. An angel of God was sent down to the mill while Ciaran was singing his psalms with purity of heart and mind, and the oats that were put in were changed, when they came out, into choice wheat.

When the grinding of the grain was finished, four sacks of consecrated wheat were found there, through the grace of God and of Ciaran. When he reached home with his wheat, he baked bread for the elders, the best that they had ever eaten. From the time that the mystical manna was found by the children of Israel, nothing like that food has ever been found. Its taste was so good with both mead and wine that it satisfied and healed them all. Every sick person in the monastery who ate it became at once perfectly whole.

While the grain was being milled, the daughter of the master of the mill arrived seeking Ciaran. She found him very attractive, for he was physically more handsome than anyone else his own age. "It is difficult, I know," said Ciaran, "but this is not what should concern you. Consider, rather, this transitory world and Judgment Day, and what you must do to avoid the pains of hell and to obtain the rewards of heaven." When the young woman had gone home, she told this to her father and to her mother. They then came and offered her to Ciaran. "If she offers her virginity to God," Ciaran said, "and if she serves him, I will be her friend for life." So the girl offered her virginity to God and to Ciaran, and all her household pledged their continual service to Ciaran.

An Exchange of Gifts

When Finnian asked Ciaran about the miracles that had happened, Ciaran told him about everything, from the beginning to the gift of the mill and of the land that had been given to him as an offering. "And all that land is for you, Finnian," said Ciaran. Finnian then gave Ciaran his blessing, and said:

O Ciaran, O little heart,
For your holiness I love you, my dear one,
Grace will come to you, my dear one.
May you have an abundance of heritage and land.

O noble Ciaran, so famous!
May every answer enrich you,
So that there is in your wonderful church
An abundance of dignity and wisdom.

So, because of Finnian's great affection for Ciaran and because of the Spirit's inspiration, Ciaran was given that special blessing. Half of the love, dignity, and wisdom regarding the people of Ireland was left to Ciaran and to his monastery.

Ciaran also left treasures with Finnian, and in his monastery those gifts are called *Ana Findein* (Finnian's treasures). The grain Ciaran gave Finnian supported Finnian's community for forty days and forty nights. A third of it was put aside for sick folk, for it healed every ailment. Neither mouse nor any other beast dared to spoil it. This grain lasted a long time, until it was finally made into a clay that healed every disease, upon whomever it was smeared.

Then, after learning scholarship and wisdom, it was time for Ciaran to leave Clonard.

The Vision of the Great Tree

Ciaran went to the island of Aran to commune with Enda. Both of them saw the same vision of a great fruitful tree growing beside a stream in the middle of Ireland. This tree protected the entire island, its fruit crossed the sea that surrounded Ireland, and the birds of the world came to carry off some of that fruit. Ciaran turned to Enda and told him what he had seen. Enda, in turn, said to him: "The great tree you saw is you, Ciaran, for you are great in the eyes of God and of all humankind. All of Ireland will be sheltered by the grace that is in you, and many people will be fed by your fasting and prayers. Go in the name of God to the center of Ireland, and found your church on the banks of a stream."

Ciaran Travels to Isel and then to Hare Island

Ciaran went to Isel to see his monastic brothers. Near Isel there was a lake, and in the lake was an island on which heathens and other rabble lived. The shouting and noise of those people used to disturb the clerics. Ciaran entreated the Lord that the island be moved from where it stood, and it was. Many people still remember that miracle, and one can still see the place in the lake where the island once was.

Now the brethren became envious of Ciaran's greatness and charity. "Go from us," they said, "for we cannot endure you any longer." So Ciaran put his books on a stag—one that used to accompany him wherever he went. This stag led him to the island of Inis Angin (Hare Island), where Ciaran decided to live for a time. Brothers from all over came to him, including a certain bishop named Daniel. This man was from Britain, and the devil encouraged him to envy Ciaran. Ciaran gave Daniel a royal cup with three golden birds as a token of his forgiveness of him. The bishop was awestruck by Ciaran's generosity, repented of his sin, and prostrated himself before Ciaran. Then he left the island.

Once when Ciaran was in Inis Angin, he heard a noise in the harbor. Speaking to the brethren, he ordered, "Go to meet him who will be your abbot." When they reached the harbor they found no one there but a heathen youth. They informed Ciaran of this. "Nevertheless," the saint said, "go back for him, since his voice has made it clear to me that it is he who will be your abbot after me." Then the young man was brought onto the island and to Ciaran. Ciaran tonsured him, and he studied with Ciaran. This was Enda Mac-Hui-Laigsi, a holy man pleasing to the Lord. He became abbot after Ciaran.

It happened that Ciaran's gospel was dropped into the lake by a certain careless brother, and it remained for a long while under the water. On a certain day in summertime cows went into the lake, and the strap of the gospel stuck to the foot of one of the cows. From beneath the waves, she brought the gospel with her dry to the harbor. When the gospel was opened, it appeared a bright shade of white, was dry, and not a letter had been destroyed. This was all due to the grace of Ciaran. To this day in Inis Angin the harbor is called Port of Sosceoil, that is, Harbor of the Gospel.

Ciaran Founds His Monastery of Clonmacnois

Three years and three months Ciaran lived on Inis Angin. After that he came to Ard Manntain, located on the banks of the Shannon. When he saw the beauty of that place he said, "If we tarry here we will have abundant wealth of the world, but few souls will go to heaven." So he moved on to Ard Tiprat (Height of the Well). "Here we will stay," he said, "for many souls will go to heaven from here, and in this place there will be communion with God and God's people forever."

On the eighth of February Ciaran set up his monastery in Cluain. Marvelous was that monastery which Ciaran set up with his eight companions after they had crossed the water—just as Noah reclaimed the world with his ark after surviving the waves of the deluge. Ciaran planted the first stake in Cluain, and Diarmait, son of Cerball, was with him. Ciaran said to Diarmait when setting the stake, "O warrior, let your hand be over my hand, and you shall have sovereignty over the men of Ireland." "I agree," Diarmait said, "provided you give me some sign." Ciaran replied, "I will promise you this: Though today you are alone, at this hour tomorrow you will be king of Ireland." Ciaran's words came true, for the king of Ireland was killed that very night, and Diarmait took the kingdom of Ireland the next day. The new king offered Ciaran a hundred churches as his own.

Ciaran's Death and Communion with Kevin

Ciaran died at the age of thirty-three. When the time of his death drew near, he said, "Let me be carried to a small height." When he looked up at the sky and the vast open air above his head, he said, "Terrible is the way of dying." "No, it cannot be terrible for you," the monks said. "Yes it is, for I do not know what commandment of God I may have transgressed," Ciaran replied, "and even David, son of Jesse, and Paul the Apostle dreaded this way."

Then angels went to meet his soul, filling as they did all the space between heaven and earth. He was carried back into his little church, and raising his hands, he blessed his people. Then he told the brethren to shut him up in the church until Kevin should come from Glendalough. After three days Kevin arrived, but he did not immediately receive the hospitality of the monks, for they were in grief and in great sorrow at Ciaran's death. Kevin cursed them, "A look of moroseness be on you always!" Great fear seized the elders, and they opened the little church to him. At once Ciaran's spirit returned from heaven and re-entered his body so that he could commune with Kevin and welcome him. The two friends stayed together from the one watch to another, engaged in mutual conversation, and strengthened their friendship. Then Ciaran blessed Kevin, and Kevin blessed water and administered the eucharist to Ciaran. Ciaran gave his bell to Kevin as a sign of their lasting unity. Today this is called *Coimgen's Boban* (Kevin's Bell).

COLUMCILLE
OF IONA

*C*olumcille, or Columba as he is known in Britain, was founder and first abbot of Iona, a tiny island located off the western coast of Scotland. He was born into a royal clan in Donegal, Ireland, December 7, 521. His name means "dove of the church." Like Ciaran, Columcille was a student of Finnian of Clonard.

After his ordination Columcille founded numerous monasteries in Ireland, including Derry in 546, Durrow in 556, and probably Kells. All of these had oak groves, the favorite trees of druids, growing on their original sites. Columcille himself is said to have addressed Christ as "my druid."

According to legends, Columcille was condemned by a synod in 561, possibly because of a copyright dispute. Whatever the reason for his exile, he left Ireland at the age of forty-two and moved to the island of Hy (Iona) in 563. A poet, scholar, and writer who obviously loved solitude, he was at the same time highly involved in pastoral ministry as head of his religious community on Iona and as a missionary to the Picts in Scotland. From the poetry and stories about him which have survived, it seems he never got over his homesickness for Ireland, especially his beloved Derry. He made at least one journey back to Ireland, visiting his monks in Durrow and other monasteries, before he died on Iona in 597.

Columcille is known as one of Ireland's greatest poets, writers, and storytellers. He is certainly one of the most talented leaders of the early Celtic church, a man of compassion and hospitality. A sixth-century poem describes him as a gentle sage "with faith in Christ" and states that "being a priest was but one of his callings." Of the monasteries associated with him, Iona has a restored medieval abbey that is home to an ecumenical community today; Kells has a number of fine high crosses and a small stone oratory; and Derry has a beautiful Long Tower Church. The most pleasing of Columcille's holy places, however, is the site at Durrow where a magnificent high cross stands serenely in the midst of ancient trees and graves. Columcille's feast day is June 9.

The Dream of Columcille's Mother and His Three Requests

Columcille's birth was foretold to Ireland's elders in visions and in dreams. His mother, Ethne, dreamed that a great cloak was given to her; this cloak reached from one part of Ireland to Scotland and contained every color of the rainbow. In her dream a youth received the radiant cloth and took the cloak from her, which caused Ethne to be very sad. Then it seemed to her that the same youth returned to her and said, "Oh, good lady, you have no need of grief or sorrow, but rather, for joy and delight. The meaning of this dream about a cloak is that you will bear a son, and Ireland and Scotland will be full of his teaching." Wonderful was the child, Columcille, who was born there, a child of the king of heaven and earth, son of Fedlimid, son of Fergus, son of Conall Bulban, son of Niall of the Nine Hostages. He was baptized by Cruthnechan, son of Cellach, the archbishop, who fostered him afterward. The angels of God had told him to do this.

Columcille offered himself to the Lord of the Elements and begged three gifts of God: chastity, wisdom, and pilgrimage. The three were fully granted to him.

Columcille Builds His Cell at Clonard and Finnian's Vision

Columcille went to Finnian of Clonard. He asked Finnian in what place he should build his cell. "Make it in front of the church," said Finnian. So Columcille built his cell there.

Each of the bishops at Clonard used to take turns grinding meal at the mill. However, an angel from heaven would grind on behalf of Columcille. That was the honor the Lord rendered to him because of the eminent nobility of his race.

Once a vision appeared to Finnian in which two moons arose from Clonard, a golden moon and a silvery moon. The golden moon went into the north of the island, lighting Ireland and Scotland. The silvery moon went on until it reached the Shannon, lighting the center of Ireland. The first, Finnian realized, foretold Columcille's wisdom and the grace of his noble kin; the second had to do with Ciaran's monastery at Clonmacnois and his many virtues and good deeds.

He Founds Monasteries at Derry and Durrow

Columcille then moved to Derry. One day he sent his monks into the forest to cut wood to build a church. The wood was cut in the territory of a certain warrior who lived near the church. He was angry that the wood was cut on his land without his own consent. When Columcille heard that, he said to his household, "Take what his wood is worth in barley-grain, and tell him to plant it in the earth." Now at that time it was past midsummer, but when the grain was taken to the warrior and he cast it into the ground, it grew and was ripe on harvest-day.

While he was in Derry, Columcille thought of going to Rome and to Jerusalem. Later, at another time, he went to Tours and brought back the gospel that had lain on Martin's breast a hundred years in the earth. That gospel was left in Derry. The Lord wrought many marvels and miracles for Columcille in Derry. He loved that city greatly, and said:

> For this do I love Derry,
> For its smoothness, for its purity,
> Because it is full of white angels
> From one end to the other.

Then Columcille went to the king of Teffia, who gave him the place today called Durrow. Columcille built a church in Durrow. When bitter apples were brought to him, he blessed them so that they became quite sweet. Columcille journeyed on to the place now called Cennannus, where he laid out the city and blessed it. There was a great oak tree under which Columcille lived while he was in that place (it remained there for many years until it fell to the ground from the force of a mighty wind). After Cennannus Columcille went on to Monasterboice.

Many, then, were the churches he marked out and the books he wrote—a total of three hundred churches and three hundred books. A book of gospels that he wrote was long under water, yet it did not have a single letter washed out.

Planting Roots on Iona and His Missionary Journeys

When Columcille had made a round of all Ireland, sowing faith and belief, he baptized many people, founded numerous churches and monasteries, and left leaders, reliquaries, and relics with each. Then the determination to go on pilgrimage, which had been with him from his earliest days, returned to his mind. So he decided to travel across the sea to preach God's word to the people of Scotland. He took with him twenty bishops, forty priests, thirty deacons, and fifty students.

With full sails he set forth until he reached the place that today is called *Hi og Colomb Cille* (Columcille's Iona). He reached it on the night of Pentecost. Two bishops who lived on the island came to expel him from it, but God revealed to Columcille that they really were not bishops. They left the island when he told them of their duplicity.

Then Columcille said to his household, "It is well for us that we plant our roots here in this soil."

When Columcille had founded Iona, he went on a preaching tour through Scotland, Britain, and Saxonland. After many miracles, and after raising the dead, he brought the people to faith and belief in Christ.

Columcille's Love of Study, Joy in Living, and Powerful Prayer

Columcille never could spend the space of even one hour without study, or prayer, or writing, or some other holy occupation. So incessantly was he engaged night and day in the exercise of fasting and watching that the burden of each of these ascetic practices would seem beyond the power of all human endurance. Still in these activities he was beloved by all, for a holy joy shown continuously on his face, revealing the joy and gladness with which the Holy Spirit filled his inmost soul. By virtue of his prayer, and in the name of our Lord Jesus Christ, he healed several persons suffering from various diseases. He alone, by the assistance of God, expelled from Iona innumerable hosts of malignant spirits. These spirits, which he saw with his own eyes, assailed him and began to bring deadly dispositions on his monastic brotherhood as well. Partly by mortification and partly by a bold resistance he subdued, with the help of Christ, the furious rage of wild beasts. The surging waves, at times rolling as high as mountains in a great storm, also quickly became at his prayer quiet and smooth, and the ship, in which he then happened to be, reached in perfect calm the haven he sought.

The Loch Ness Monster

One time when Columcille was living for some days in the province of the Picts, he was obliged to cross the river Ness. When he reached the bank of the river, he saw some of the inhabitants burying an unfortunate man who, according to the account of those who were burying him, had been seized a short time before as he was swimming and been bitten most severely by a monster that lived in the water. His wretched body was taken out with a hook by those who came to his assistance in a boat. Columcille, on hearing this, directed one of his companions to swim over and row across the cable that was moored at the farther bank. Lugne Mocumin obeyed without the least delay, taking off all his clothes except his tunic and leaping into the water. But the monster, far from being satiated, was only roused for more prey. Lying at the bottom of the stream, it felt the water disturbed above by the man swimming, and so suddenly rose to the surface. Giving an awful roar, it plunged after him, with its mouth wide open, as the man swam in the middle of the stream.

Columcille observed this, raised his holy hand—while all the rest, brethren as well as strangers, were stupefied with terror— and invoking the name of God formed the saving sign of the cross in the air. He commanded the ferocious monster, saying to it, "You will go no further; do not touch the man; go back with all speed."

At the voice of the saint, the monster was terrified and fled more quickly than if it had been pulled back with ropes, though it had just gotten so near to Lugne that there was not more than the length of a spear between the man and the beast. Seeing that the monster had gone back, and that their comrade Lugne returned to them safe and sound, the companions were struck with admiration and gave glory to God in the holy man. Even the strangers who were present were forced by the greatness of

---

this miracle, which they themselves had seen, to glorify the God of the Christians.

His Miracles and Companionship with Angels

While returning from the country of the Picts, where he had been for some days, Columcille hoisted his sail when the breeze was against him in order to confound the druids, and he made as rapid a voyage as if the wind had truly been favorable. On other occasions contrary winds were changed into fair because of his prayers. In that same country he took a white stone from the river and blessed it for the working of certain cures; contrary to the law of nature, that stone floated like an apple when placed in water. This divine miracle was performed in the presence of King Bruded and his household.

In the same country Columcille also performed a still greater miracle by raising to life the dead child of a humble believer and restoring him in life and vigor to his father and mother. At another time, while the blessed man was yet a young deacon in Ireland and living with the holy bishop Findbarr of Cork, the wine required for the sacred mysteries failed, and through his prayer, Columcille changed pure water into true wine. An immense blaze of heavenly light was on many occasions seen by some of the brothers to surround Columcille in the light of day as well as in the darkness of night. He was also favored with the sweet and most delightful company of holy angels. The Holy Spirit often revealed to him the souls of some just people carried by angels to the highest heavens, as well as certain reprobates being carried to hell by demons. Columcille frequently foretold the future of many persons, sometimes joyful and sometimes sad, while they were still living.

The Story of the Crane

While Columcille was living on Iona, he called one of the brothers to him and said: "Three days from now, in the morning, you must sit down and wait for a crane on the shore on the western side of this island. A stranger from the northern region of Ireland, it has been driven about by various winds. This crane will come, weary and fatigued, after the ninth hour. It will lie down before you on the beach quite exhausted. Treat that bird tenderly and take it to some nearby house where you can kindly and carefully nurse it and feed it for three days and three nights. When the crane is refreshed after three days of rest and is no longer willing to stay with us, it will fly back with renewed strength to the pleasant part of Ireland from which it originally came. I entrust this bird to you with special care because it comes from our native land."

The brother obeyed Columcille, and on the third day, after the ninth hour, he watched as he had been told for the arrival of the expected guest. As soon as the crane came and alighted on the shore, he gently picked up the weak and hungry bird and carried it to a dwelling that was nearby, where he fed it. On the man's return to the monastery that evening, Columcille, without inquiry but rather as if stating a fact, said to him, "God bless you, my son, for your kind attention to this foreign visitor. It will not remain here for very long, but will return within three days to its old home."

It happened exactly as the saint predicted, for after being nursed carefully for three days, the bird flapped its wings and gently rose to a great height in the sight of its hospitable host. Then, on that calm day, it made its way through the air homeward, flying straight across the sea to Ireland.

Angelic Light on a Winter's Night

One winter's night a monk named Virgnous, burning with the love of God, entered the church alone to pray. The others were asleep. He prayed fervently in a little side chamber attached to the walls of the oratory. After about an hour, the venerable Columcille entered the same sacred house. Along with him, at the same time, a golden light came down from the highest heavens and filled that part of the church. Even the separate recess of the side chamber, where Virgnous was attempting to hide himself as much as he could, was also filled, to his great alarm, with some of the brilliance of that heavenly light. As no one can look directly at or gaze with steady eye on the summer sun in its midday splendor, so Virgnous could not at all bear the heavenly brightness he saw because the brilliant and unspeakable radiance overpowered his sight. This brother, in fact, was so terrified by the splendor, almost as dreadful as lightning, that no strength remained in him. Finally, after a short prayer, St. Columcille left the church.

The next day he sent for Virgnous, who was very much alarmed, and spoke to him these consoling words: "You are crying to good purpose, my child, for last night you were very pleasing in the sight of God by keeping your eyes fixed on the ground when you were overwhelmed with fear at the brightness. If you had not done that, son, the bright light would have blinded your eyes. You must never, however, disclose this great manifestation of light while I live."

This incident, therefore, so wonderful and so worthy of recording, became known to many only after the saint's death through this same Virgnous.

Columcille's Approaching Death and the White Horse

A true prophet, Columcille knew long before his death when he would die. One day during the month of May the old man, worn out with age, went in a chariot to visit some of the brethren who were at work. When he had found them on the western side of Iona, he began to speak to them, saying, "With great yearning during the Paschal solemnities this past April, I desired to depart to Christ the Lord, and he gave me permission to do so, if I wished. But rather than have a joyous feast turned for you into mourning, I thought it better to put off for a little longer the time of my departure from the world." The beloved monks hearing this sad news were greatly affected, but he tried as well as he could to cheer them with words of consolation. Then, having done this, he turned his face to the east, still seated as he was in his chariot, and blessed the island with its inhabitants. From that day to the present, the venomous reptiles with the three-forked tongues could not harm man or beast.

On his way back to the monastery, Columcille rested half way at a place where a cross was later erected. The cross is standing to this day, fixed into a millstone, and can be observed on the roadside. While the saint, bowed down with old age, sat there to rest a little, a white packhorse came up to him. It was the same willing servant that used to carry the milk vessels from the cowshed to the monastery. As it came up to the saint, it laid its head on his bosom—inspired by God to do so, since each animal is gifted with the knowledge of things according to the will of the Creator. Somehow knowing that its master was about to leave, and that it would see him no more, this white horse began to neigh plaintively and, like a human being, to shed copious tears on the saint's chest. When his attendant saw this, he began to drive the weeping mourner away, but the saint forbade him, saying: "Let it be, Diormit. Since it is so fond of me, let it shed its tears of grief on my chest. Consider this: since you are human and have a rational soul, you cannot know anything of my departure, except what I myself have just told you. But to this humble beast, devoid of reason, the Creator himself has evidently in some way revealed that its master is about to leave it." Saying this, the saint blessed the horse, which sadly turned away from him.

Columcille's Death and the Calming of the Sea

Leaving this spot, Columcille climbed the hill that overlooks the monastery and stood for some little time on its summit. As he stood there with both hands uplifted, he blessed his monastery, saying: "Small and humble though this place is, yet it will be held in great and unusual honor, not only by Scottish kings and people, but also by the rulers of foreign and barbarous nations and by their subjects. Even the saints of other churches will regard it with great reverence." After these words he descended the hill and returned to the monastery, where he sat in his cell transcribing the Psalter. When he came to that verse of Psalm 34, where it is written, "Those who seek the Lord will desire nothing," he said: "At the end of the page, I must stop. What follows let Baithene write." Indeed Baithene succeeded Columcille, as was recommended by him, not only in teaching, but also in writing.

When Columcille had written the verse at the end of the page, he went to the church to the nocturnal vigils of the Lord's Day. As soon as this was over, he returned to his room and spent the rest of the night on his bed, where he had a bare quilt for his couch, and for his pillow a stone, which stands to this day as a kind of monument beside his grave. While reclining there, he gave his last instruction to the brethren in the hearing of his attendant alone: "These, O my children, are the last words I address to you: be at peace, and have genuine charity among yourselves. If you follow the example of the holy fathers, God, the comforter of all good, will be your helper, and I, abiding with him, will intercede for you. He will not only give you enough to supply the needs of this present life, but will also bestow on you the good and eternal rewards which are laid up for those that keep his commandments."

After these words, as the happy hour of his departure gradually approached, the saint became silent. When the bell tolled at midnight, he rose and went to the church. Running more quickly than the rest, he entered it alone and knelt down in prayer beside the altar. At the same moment his attendant Diormit, who followed him more slowly, saw from a distance that the whole interior of the church was filled with a heavenly light in the direction of the saint. As he drew near to the door, the same light he had seen, and which was also seen by a few more of the brethren standing at a distance, quickly disappeared.

Diormit entered the church and cried out mournfully, "Where are you, father?" Feeling his way in the darkness, since the brethren had not yet brought in the lights, he found the saint lying before the altar. Raising Columcille up a little, Diormit sat down beside him and laid his holy head on his bosom.

Meanwhile the rest of the monks arrived with their lights, and seeing their dying father, burst into lamentations. The saint, opened his eyes wide and looked round him from side to side with a countenance full of wonderful joy and gladness, no doubt seeing the holy angels coming to meet him. Diormit then raised the holy right hand of the saint, so that he might bless his assembled monks. The venerable father himself moved his hand at the same time, as well as he could. Having blessed them in this way, he immediately breathed his last. After his soul had left the tabernacle of the body, his face continued to shine, brightened in a wonderful way by his vision of the angels, to such a degree that he had the appearance not so much of one dead as of one alive and sleeping. Meanwhile the whole church resounded with loud lamentations of grief.

When his holy soul had departed and the matin hymns were finished, his sacred body was carried by the brethren, chanting psalms, from the church back to his room. His obsequies were celebrated with all due honor and reverence for three days and as many nights. When these sweet praises of God were ended, his venerable body was wrapped in a clean shroud of fine linen and placed in the coffin prepared for it. He was buried with all due veneration, to rise again with lustrous and eternal brightness.

———

During the three days and nights of his obsequies, there arose a storm of wind without rain. It blew so violently that it prevented every one from crossing the sound. Immediately after the internment of the holy man, the storm stopped at once, the wind ceased, and the whole sea became calm.

CUTHBERT

OF LINDISFARNE

FARNE ISLAND

Cuthbert is considered northern England's most popular saint and one of Christianity's greatest spiritual guides. He was a monk and bishop of Lindisfarne, where Aidan had settled when he journeyed from Iona and founded his monastic community. Although little is known about Cuthbert's early life, he was probably born about 634 into a fairly well-to-do Anglo-Saxon family somewhere near the River Tweed in southern Scotland. Despite his Saxon origins, he was very much a Celt by temperament and deeply influenced by Celtic spirituality. The monks of Durham, where his relics eventually found a home, claimed that he was of royal Irish blood and was probably born in Ireland. An Irish hagiography of the saint even professed that his mother was an Irish princess called Sabina and that after her father's death, she entered a monastery at Kells, where Cuthbert was born.

In 651 Cuthbert joined the Celtic monastery at Melrose. In 676, after twenty-five years of intense pastoral involvement with the local people, as well as serving as guestmaster at Ripon and prior at Lindisfarne, Cuthbert moved to Inner Farne Island, not far from Lindisfarne. There he attempted to live as a solitary. After building a cell and settling into his own soul-making, however, great numbers of people sought him out for spiritual guidance. In 684, against his own wishes, he was elected a bishop, but only agreed to accept that office after the king himself sailed to his island retreat and begged him to do so. The following year Cuthbert was consecrated bishop of Lindisfarne, and once again assumed a very active ministry. In 687 he resigned as bishop and returned to his beloved Inner Farne, where he died.

Bede's stories about Cuthbert portray a humble and joyful saint who successfully handled the tension between his love of people and passion for solitude. He is buried behind the high altar in Durham Cathedral, one of England's most beautiful churches. Bede's tomb is at the opposite end of the church, in the Galilee Chapel. It seems fitting that these two, who had so much in common, share a common place of pilgrimage. Cuthbert's feast day is celebrated March 20.

Cuthbert's Childhood

When Cuthbert was a child, he was privileged to see and talk with an angel. One time his knee suddenly began to hurt. A great tumor swelled up, causing the muscles of his kneecap to contract. At first he was able to hop with his foot off the ground, but eventually the swelling increased so that he could hardly walk at all. One day the servants carried him outside to lie in the fresh air. Looking up he saw a horseman approaching from a great distance. The man was dressed in white, with a noble appearance, and riding a horse of unparalleled beauty. The man rode up, saluted Cuthbert courteously, and asked, almost jokingly, if he would mind ministering to such a guest as himself. Cuthbert replied: "I am only too willing to show you hospitality, but I am unable to do so because of this disease of my leg. For a long time now I have been troubled with it, and there is no doctor anywhere with enough skill to cure it."

The horseman got down from his horse, looked intently at the knee, and ordered, "Boil some wheat flour in milk and bathe the tumor with it hot, and you will be healed." Then he mounted and rode off.

Cuthbert did as he was told and within a few days was well again. He knew that it was an angel that had given him the remedy, sent by the same power who had sent the Archangel Raphael to cure Tobias' eyes. This appearance of an angel on horseback reflects the history of the Maccabees, where angels on horseback come to defend both Judas Maccabaeus and the Temple itself.

From then on the boy devoted himself to God, and as he would later tell his friends, when he prayed for help against frequent and pressing difficulties, he frequently had angels sent to defend him. Cuthbert was heard by God, who listens to the cry of the poor and delivers them from all their tribulations, because he in turn was kind enough to pray for others in similar dangers.

Cuthbert's Discernment of Vocation

Cuthbert was up in the hills tending a flock of sheep committed to his charge. One night when his companions had gone to sleep and he was keeping watch and praying as was his custom, he suddenly saw light streaming from the skies, breaking the long night's darkness, and choirs of angels coming down to earth. These angelic hosts quickly took a human soul, shining brightly, into their ranks. Then they returned to their home above. Cuthbert was so moved by this vision that he decided to give himself to spiritual discipline in order to gain eternal happiness with the powerful people of God.

Immediately he began to thank God and in a brotherly way to exhort his companions to praise him. "How wretched we are, given up to sleep and laziness so that we never see the glory of those who watch with Christ unceasingly! What miraculous things I have seen after so short a vigil! The gate of heaven opened and a band of angels led in the spirit of some holy man. While we are still in deepest darkness, that man has the happiness of forever looking on the halls of heaven and their king. I believe that he must have been some sort of holy bishop or layman of great distinction, since he was led in with such splendor and light by numerous angels."

Thus Cuthbert made the hearts of the shepherds excited about the love and honor of God. The next day he was told that Aidan, bishop of Lindisfarne, a man of outstanding holiness, had passed into heaven at the time of his vision. Cuthbert returned the sheep to their owners and decided to enter a monastery.

Cuthbert's Mentor, Boisil, at Melrose

Encouraged by his heavenly vision of the joys of eternal happiness, Cuthbert was ready to suffer hunger and thirst in this life in order to enjoy the banquets of the next. He was aware that the community of Lindisfarne was filled with holy monks, under whose example and teaching he might make good progress. It was, however, a priest of Melrose by the name of Boisil and his reputation for extraordinary virtue that led Cuthbert to enter there. By chance Boisil was standing at the monastery gates when the young man arrived and thus saw him first. Cuthbert dismounted, gave his horse and spear to a servant, and went to the church to pray. Boisil intuited the high degree of holiness to which the boy would rise and said just a single phrase to the monks with whom he was standing, "Behold the servant of the Lord." In that way, he imitated him who, at the approach of Nathaniel, exclaimed, "Behold an Israelite indeed, one in whom there is no guile."

Boisil said no more, but graciously welcomed Cuthbert. When the latter had explained the purpose of his visit—to leave the world behind him—Boisil received him with great kindness into the community. A few days later the priest Eata arrived. At that time Eata was abbot of Melrose; later he became abbot and bishop of Lindisfarne. Boisil told him about Cuthbert, explained how well disposed he was, and gained permission for him to receive the tonsure and become one of the community.

Once Cuthbert was admitted, he was careful to keep up with the rest in observing the rule. He excelled them, however, in zeal for strict discipline, and he watched, prayed, worked, and read harder than anyone else. Like Samson the Nazarite he carefully abstained from all alcoholic drink. Still, he was not too severe with himself regarding the food he ate, since he did not want his work to suffer. Cuthbert was robust and strong, fit enough to carry out everything to which he put his hand.

Cuthbert's Self-Disclosure and the Death of His Mentor

A few years later when King Alhfrith, in order to save his soul, gave Abbot Eata ground at Ripon to build a monastery, the abbot transferred some of the monks there, under the same rule as they had at Melrose. Cuthbert was one of them, and he was appointed guestmaster. Angels would frequently appear and converse with him, and when he was hungry he would be refreshed with food by the special gift of God.

Cuthbert was a very pleasant, affable man. He generally restricted himself to citing the lives of the fathers when he wanted to find models of holy living for his brother-monks. At times, however, he would mention his own spiritual graces in all humility. Sometimes he did this openly; sometimes he talked in the third person as though it were someone else. His audience always knew that he was speaking like St. Paul, who often would recount his virtues openly, and at other times as though speaking of another as when he said: "I knew a man in Christ, about fourteen years ago, such a person caught up even to the seventh heaven" (2 Cor 12:2).

Cuthbert enthusiastically followed the words and actions of Boisil. One time he was struck down by a plague, which was ravaging up and down the countryside. When Cuthbert was better, Boisil prophesied that he would never again be afflicted by the same illness. "At the same time," said Boisil, "I warn you not to lose the chance of learning from me, for death is close to me. By next week my body and voice shall have lost their strength."

Cuthbert knew that Boisil was telling the truth, and said, "Then tell me what is the best book to study, one that can be got through in a week."

"St. John the Evangelist," Boisil answered. "I have a commentary in seven parts. With the help of God we can read one a day and perhaps discuss it if we want."

It was done as Boisil said. They were able to finish quickly because they did not discuss the profound arguments but the simple things of "the faith that works by love." On the seventh day, when the reading was finished, illness overtook Boisil, and he entered into the joy of eternal bliss. He is believed to have told Cuthbert all about his future during that week, for he was a prophet and a very holy man.

Cuthbert's Administrative and Pastoral Ministries

On Boisil's death Cuthbert became prior at Melrose, an office which he enthusiastically held for many years. In the monastery he counseled the monks on the religious life and set a high example of it himself; outside, in the world, he tried to convert people for miles around from their foolish ways to a delight in the promised joys of heaven. Many Christians had profaned their faith by their actions. While the plague was raging, some had forgotten the mystery given to them in baptism and fled to idols— as if incantations or amulets or any other diabolical rubbish could possibly help them. To bring back both kinds of sinners Cuthbert often did the rounds of the villages, sometimes on horseback, more often on foot, preaching the way of truth to those who had gone astray. Boisil had done the same in his time, as had Aidan.

Among the English people at that time, it was customary that if a priest or cleric came to a village everyone would obey his call and gather to hear him preach. They would willingly listen and even more happily put his words into practice as far as they understood them. So exceptional was Cuthbert's skill in teaching and his ability to make a point, and so gloriously did his face shine like an angel's, that no one dared keep from him even the greatest secrets of his or her heart. They openly confessed every sin (for they truly believed that he would know if they held anything back!) and made amends by "fruits worthy of repentance," as he commanded. Cuthbert frequently visited even those steep rugged places in the hills that other preachers dreaded to approach because of their poverty and squalor. This, to Cuthbert, was a labor of love. He was so eager to preach that sometimes he would be away for a whole week, two weeks, or even a month, living with the rough hill folk, preaching, and calling them to heaven by his example.

His Friendship with Women, and How Otters Warmed His Feet

Inside the monastery Cuthbert performed more and more signs and wonders, and his reputation increased. A certain nun called Aebbe was in charge of the convent of Coldingham. Aebbe was honored for both her piety and her nobility, for she was King Oswy's sister. One day she sent a message to Cuthbert asking if he would come and exhort the community. The holy man came and stayed a few days, showing them the way of salvation in deed and in word.

It was Cuthbert's custom to rise in the dead of night, while everyone else was sleeping, and to go out and pray, returning just in time for morning prayers. One night a monk watched him sneak out, and then secretly followed him to see where he was going and what he was about. Cuthbert went down toward the beach below the monastery and out into the sea until he was up to his arms and neck in deep water. Waves splashed all during his vigil throughout the dark hours of the night. At daybreak Cuthbert came out of the water, knelt down on the sand, and prayed. Suddenly two otters jumped out of the sea, stretched themselves out before him, warmed his feet with their breath, and even tried to dry him with their fur. When they had finished, they received his blessing and slipped back to their watery home. Soon he was home and back in choir with the rest of the monks at the proper time.

One day during his travels Cuthbert came to the house of a holy woman who was known for her good works. He often visited her because she was his old nurse; in fact, he always called her Mother. This woman lived west of the village. No sooner had he entered the place than a house in the eastern quarter of the town caught fire through carelessness and began to blaze. A wind sprang up, from the same direction, tore away portions of blazing straw from the roof, and scattered them far and wide. As the fire got hotter it kept back the men who were attempting to throw water on it, finally forcing them to retreat. This holy woman, filled with fear, ran back to her home to find Cuthbert and implore him to pray; otherwise the whole village would be destroyed, and her house along with it. "Do not worry, Mother, keep calm," Cuthbert told her. He then went out and lay full length on the ground in front of the door. Before he had finished praying, the wind had changed to the west, putting the house Cuthbert had entered completely out of danger.

Cuthbert's Zeal for Prayer and Tears of Compassion

When the respected servant of God had lived many years in the monastery at Melrose, where he had distinguished himself by many signs of spiritual power, Abbot Eata transferred him to the monastery at Lindisfarne. Cuthbert was sent as prior to teach the true rule of monastic life and to illustrate it by his own perfect example. When he came to the church and monastery of Lindisfarne, he kept up his custom of frequent visits to the common people in the neighborhood, so as to encourage them to seek and to be worthy of the rewards of heaven. Cuthbert became famous for miracles, for his prayers healed all kinds of disease and affliction. He cured some people who were harassed by unclean spirits by laying his hands directly on them, exhorting and exorcising them. Others he healed from a great distance, merely by praying or predicting their cure.

Such was Cuthbert's zeal for prayer that sometimes, it was rumored, he would keep vigil for three or four nights straight, without ever sleeping in his bed. Whether praying alone in some secret place or saying his psalms, he always did manual work to drive away the heaviness of sleep. Other times he would travel round the island and kindly inquire how things were going, relieving the tedium of his long vigils and psalm-singing by walking about.

Cuthbert was so filled with sorrow for sin, and so aflame with heavenly yearnings, that he could never finish Mass without shedding tears. As was only fitting, he would imitate the sacred ritual that he was celebrating by offering himself to God with a contrite heart. His people were encouraged to lift their hearts and give thanks to the Lord God more by the yearnings of his own heart than by the sound of his voice, more by his sighs than by his preaching. He readily challenged wrongdoers because of his thirst for justice, but his gentleness made him quick to forgive penitents. Often he would be the first to burst into tears, tears of compassion, as they were pouring out their sins. Though he himself did not need to do so, he would show them how to make recompense for their sins by doing the penance himself. He wore ordinary clothes which were neither remarkably neat nor noticeably dirty. For many years the monastery followed his example. The monks were discouraged from wearing expensive dyed cloth and were expected to be content with natural wool.

Cuthbert's Search for Solitude

At last, after many years living in the monastery, Cuthbert entered joyfully and with the goodwill of the abbot and monks into that remoter solitude he had so long sought after, thirsted for, and prayed for. He was exceedingly happy that after a long and spotless active life he should be considered worthy to ascend to the stillness of divine contemplation.

In order to learn the first steps of the hermit's life, he retired to a more solitary place in the outer precincts of the monastery. Only after he had gained victory over the devil through prayer and fasting did he take it upon himself to seek a remote battlefield farther away from his colleagues. The Farne is an island far out to sea, unlike Lindisfarne, which strictly speaking is an island only twice a day, when it is cut off by the tide. The Farne lies a few miles to the southeast of Lindisfarne, and is cut off on the landward side by very deep water and, on the other side, faces out toward the limitless ocean. This island was haunted by devils, and Cuthbert was the first man brave enough to live there alone. When he had routed the enemy, he built a structure almost circular in plan, from four to five poles in diameter, with the walls on the outside higher than a man. There were two buildings, a small church and another for living in. Cuthbert finished the walls inside and out by digging away a lot of the soil. The roofs were of roughhewn timber and straw. Near the landing there was a bigger house for visiting monks, with a spring nearby.

Cuthbert's dwelling place, built on almost solid rock, had no water supply. So one day Cuthbert summoned the brethren (for he had not yet cut himself off from his visitors) and said: "As you can see, the place I have chosen lacks a well. Pray with me, I beg you, so that God may open a spring of water for us." They dug a pit and the next morning found it full of water gushing up from underneath. No doubt it was the prayers of the saint that had brought forth water from the driest, hardest kind of soil.

Once the brethren had helped him to build the place, Cuthbert lived completely alone, shutting himself within the hermitage. Thus he learned to live a hermit's life of prayer and fasting.

Cuthbert as a Confessor and Spiritual Guide

Great numbers of people, attracted by his reputation for miracles, came to Cuthbert at the Farne—not just from Lindisfarne but even from the remote parts of Britain. They confessed their sins, confided in him about their temptations, and acknowledged to him the common troubles of humanity they were laboring under—all in the hope of gaining consolation from so holy a man. They were not disappointed. No one left unconsoled; no one had to carry back the burdens with which he or she had come. He could warm spirits chilled with sadness to hope with a comforting word. He could bring those who were overcome with anxiety to thoughts of the joys of heaven. Cuthbert revealed to them that both good fortune and bad were transitory in this world. To those who were afflicted with temptation he would skillfully disclose all the cleverness of the devil and explain that a soul lacking in love for God or humanity is easily caught in the devil's snares, while one that is strong in faith can, with God's help, brush them aside like so many spiders' webs.

Cuthbert frequently emphasized that people should not marvel at his way of life, as though it were especially exalted. "You ought to stand in awe of the monastic lifestyle, for in that life everything is subject to the abbot. I have known many abbots who have far surpassed my poor self by their purity of mind and the depth of their prophetic power—Boisil, for example, was such a man to be honored and venerated. He was old and I but a youth when he brought me up in the monastery of Melrose. While he was teaching me, he accurately prophesied my whole future. One of those prophecies, however, has yet to happen; would to God it might not."

Here Cuthbert referred to Boisil's prophecy that he would someday be a bishop. His desire for a more secluded life made him tremble at the thought.

Cuthbert Becomes Bishop and Later Returns to Inner Farne

Not much later there was a great synod presided over by Archbishop Theodore of Canterbury in the presence of King Ecgfrith. At it Cuthbert, by general consent, was elected bishop of Lindisfarne. Letters and messengers were repeatedly sent to him, but he refused to move. Finally the king himself and that most holy bishop, Trumwine, sailed across with numerous devout and influential officials, knelt down, and earnestly entreated him in the name of the Lord. They wept and pleaded with him until at last he came forth from his beloved hiding place, his eyes filled with tears, and was taken to the synod. Very reluctantly he yielded to their unanimous decision and submitted to the yoke of the episcopacy.

In the second year of his episcopate Cuthbert knew that his end was near. He laid aside his pastoral duties and as soon as possible went back to his beloved life as a solitary. He was given almost two months to rediscover the delights of the quiet life before being suddenly felled by disease.

Cuthbert's Death

"When I went in to him about the ninth hour," the priest Herefrith said, "I found him lying in a corner of the oratory opposite the altar. I sat down beside him. He said very little, since it was hard for him to speak. When I asked him rather urgently what advice he was going to leave us as his last testament, however, he launched into a brief but significant discourse on peace

---

and humility: "Always preserve divine charity among yourselves, and when you come together to discuss your common affairs let your principal goal be to reach a unanimous decision. Live in mutual harmony with all other servants of Christ. Do not despise those faithful who come to you seeking hospitality. Receive them, put them up, and set them on their way with kindness, treating them as one of yourselves. Do not ever think yourselves better than the rest of your companions who share the same faith and follow the monastic life."

Cuthbert passed the day quietly until evening and peacefully continued praying throughout the night. Then, strengthened by the eucharist in preparation for the death he knew was now imminent, he raised his eyes to heaven, stretched his arms aloft, and with his mind praising the Lord sent forth his spirit to the joy of paradise.

DAVID

O F   W A L E S

david, or Dewi Sant as the Welsh call him, is the patron saint of Wales. He was born about 520, the son of Sanctus, a Welsh king, and Non, one of the great female saints of the early Celtic church. David became the founder of numerous monasteries, including the monastery called Cell Muine in the southwestern corner of Wales. (The town where the monastery was located now bears his name.)

David appears in numerous Celtic hagiographies as a soul friend and mentor of many saints, including Maedoc of Ferns. Such famous Irish monastic founders as Finnian of Clonard, Senan of Scattery Island, Findbarr of Cork, and Brendan of Clonfert visited him at his Welsh monastery. David himself, according to his hagiographer, was a pilgrim to Jerusalem, where he went with two other saints to be consecrated archbishop. Although the story is probably historically inaccurate, it does refer to the highly popular practice of pilgrimage to the Holy Land during medieval times. It also expresses the hagiographer's attempt to portray St. David's bishop-successors in the eleventh century as politically and religiously independent of church leaders in Canterbury and Rome.

David was nicknamed the Waterman, probably because of the strict monastic rule, including abstinence from alcohol, which he enforced at his Welsh monastery. Still, despite his asceticism and hard work, his spirituality was evidently not devoid of happiness, especially when we take into account his last words to his community and neighbors. Day-to-day life in his monastery, which is recounted in the stories about him, can be considered "real history," according to scholar E. G. Bowen; they provide us with "the best and most vivid description of life in an early Celtic Christian monastery that we possess."

David died in either 589 or 601. Years after his death his body was transferred from the rustic monastery church to the grand Saint David's Cathedral, where his relics can be seen today. Gerald of Wales, the peripatetic medieval churchman, pilgrim, and storyteller is also entombed there. St. David's feast day is celebrated March 1.

Prophecy of David's Greatness

Although our Lord has loved and known his own before ever he created the world, there are some whom he makes known beforehand by many signs and revelations. That saint who was named David in his baptism, but Dewi by the common people, was not only foretold by authentic prophecies of angels thirty years before his birth (first to his father, and then to St. Patrick), but was also proclaimed as one who was enriched with mystic gifts and endowments.

On a certain occasion his father, Sanctus by name and merits, and in full enjoyment of royal power over the people of Ceredigion, heard in a dream the voice of an angel forewarning him: "Tomorrow you will awake and go hunting. You will kill a stag near the river, and in that place you will find three gifts, namely, the stag you will pursue, a fish, and a hive of bees. Now, of these three, you will set aside the honeycomb and a portion of the fish and of the stag. These you will send to Maucannus's monastery, there to be preserved for a son who will be born of you." These three gifts foreshadowed David's life. The honeycomb declared his wisdom, for just as the honey lies embedded in the wax, so he perceived the spiritual meaning within a literal statement. The fish proclaimed his abstinence, for as the fish lives by water, so David rejected wine, fermented liquor, and everything intoxicating. He led a blessed life for God on bread and water only; thus he was called "David who lives on water." The stag signified his power over the ancient serpent. For as the stag, after feeding on the snakes it has destroyed, longs for a spring of water, so David selected his own well of life with a ceaseless flow of tears.

David's Childhood, Ordination,
and Healing of His Teacher

After his birth, David was baptized by Ailbe, a bishop of the Munstermen. A spring of very clear water suddenly burst forth at that spot, which provided the waters for his baptism. The child miraculously opened the eyes of blind Movi, who held him and whose eyes the water splashed, revealing to him the light of day he had never known.

The boy was then reared in the place called Vetus Rubus, and he grew up full of grace, and pleasing to behold. There he was taught his letters, and learned the church practices, and his fellow pupils saw a dove teaching him and singing hymns with him. As time passed his virtues and his merits increased, and, keeping his body free from a wife's embraces, he was ordained to the dignity of a priest. He then left there and went to live with Paulinus on an island. This Paulinus was a disciple of Germanus and a teacher who led a life pleasing to God.

Holy Dewi remained there many years, reading and fully assimilating what he read. It so happened that Paulinus was troubled with his eyes during that time. He called the students together and asked that each bless his eyes and touch them, so that they might be healed by the prayers and blessings. After the other pupils had taken their turn touching the master's eyes and signing them with the sign of the cross, holy Dewi was asked to do so. He, however, replied: "Until now I have never looked into my master's face. For although I have been here reading with him for ten years, I have never seen his countenance." For David had been overwhelmed with shyness and modesty. Then his master said to him, "Without looking, raise your hand and touch my eyes, and I shall be healed." When David had done this, the light of day was clearly revealed to his teacher, darkness was driven from his eyes, and he regained that sight of which he had been deprived. Thanks were then given to God, and holy Dewi was indeed praised and blessed by one and all.

David Founds His Monasteries

David left Paulinus and founded twelve monasteries. First he reached Glastonbury in England and built a church. Next he went to Bath, where he changed the foul water to healthy by blessing it, endowing it with a continuous heat that made it suitable for the bathing of bodies. Afterward he founded other monasteries in different locales. These monasteries he founded in the usual way, distributing to each the articles required by canonical order and laying down the rules of monastic conduct.

He then returned to the place he had left behind when he set forth on his journeying. His uncle, Bishop Guisdianus, lived there. When they were bringing solace to each other in holy conversation, Dewi said to him, "My angel companion has told me, 'From the place where you intend to serve God, scarcely one out of every hundred will gain his heavenly reward. But there is another place nearby, where scarcely one of those buried in the cemetery in the saving faith will pay the penalties of hell.'"

One day his three most faithful disciples, Aidan, Eliud, and Ismael, came to David. They were accompanied by a group of their fellow disciples. One in mind and heart, they went to a place previously foretold by an angel where, in the name of God, they lit a fire. The smoke lifted high into the sky and filled and encircled the whole island as well as Ireland. There at Menevia, on the site the angel had previously shown them, the community built a noble monastery in the Lord's name. When this was all completed, such an asceticism did David decree in his zeal for the monastic system that every monk toiled at daily labor and spent his life working with his hands for the community. "For who does not work," says the apostle, "let him not eat" (2 Thes 3:10). Knowing that idle rest was the source and the mother of vices David bowed down the shoulders of the monks with pious labors, for those who give in to idleness develop a spirit of instability and apathy with restless lustful urges.

The Daily Routine of the Monastery

David's monks eagerly worked with feet and hands. They placed the yoke upon their shoulders, dug the earth unweariedly with mattocks and spades, and carried in their holy hands hoes and saws for cutting. With their own efforts, they provided for all the necessities of the community. They scorned possessions, rejected the gifts of the wicked, and abhorred riches. They brought in no oxen to help themselves or the brethren. No complaint was heard; in fact, there was no conversation beyond

---

that which was necessary. Each one performed his task prayerfully and meditatively.

When labor in the fields was finished they returned to the cloisters of the monastery and spent the whole of the day until the evening in reading, writing, or praying. When evening came, and the stroke of the bell sounded, whether only the tip of a letter or even half the form of the same letter was written, they rose quickly and left what they were doing. In silence, without empty talk or chatter, they went to the church. When they finished chanting the psalms, with voice and heart in complete harmony, they humbled themselves on bended knees until the appearance of the stars in the heavens brought the day to a close. After they left the church, the father remained alone to pour forth his prayer to God in secret for the welfare of the church.

At length they assembled at table. Every one restored and refreshed his weary limbs by partaking of supper, but not to excess, for too much, though it be of bread alone, engenders self-indulgence. All took supper according to the varying conditions of their bodies or age. They did not serve courses of different flavors, or the richer kinds of food; their food was bread and herbs seasoned with salt, while they quenched a burning thirst with a temperate kind of drink. For the sick, those advanced in age, or those wearied by a long journey, they provided some dishes of tastier food.

When thanks had been returned to God, they went to the church in accordance with canonical rule, and there they gave themselves up to watchings, prayers, and genuflections for about three hours. While they were praying in the church, no one dared to yawn, no one to sneeze, no one to spit.

Then they composed their limbs for sleep. Waking up at cock-crow, they applied themselves to prayer on bended knees and spent the remainder of the night until morning without sleep. In the same way they served throughout the other nights. From Saturday evening until daybreak at the first hour of Sunday, they gave themselves to watchings, prayers, and genuflections, except for one hour after matins on Saturday.

They also revealed their thoughts to the father and obtained his permission even for the requirements of nature. All things were in common; there was no "mine" or "thine," for whoever should say "my book" or "my anything else" was immediately subject to a severe penance. They wore clothes of simple quality, mainly made from animal skins. There was unfailing obedience to the father's command. Great was their perseverance in the performance of duties; great was their uprightness in all things.

It was the custom that anyone who yearned for this manner of saintly life and asked to join this monastic community first remained for ten days at the door of the monastery, as if rejected and also silenced by words of abuse. If he put his patience to good use and stood there until the tenth day, he might be admitted and first put to serve under the elder who had charge of the gate. After he had toiled there for a long time, and many conflicts within his soul had been reconciled, he was finally judged fit to enter the brethren's society.

There was no superfluity. Voluntary poverty was loved, for David accepted nothing for the use of the monastery of any entrant's worldly wealth—not even one penny. Naked, as though escaping from a shipwreck, candidates were received, so that they should not in any way extol themselves or esteem themselves above the brethren, or on grounds of wealth refuse an equal share of toil. Further, if anyone decided to leave the monastery, there was no way that person could forcibly extort what he had left behind, thus turning the monks' patience into anger.

David's Ascetic Practices in Imitation of the Desert Monks

David himself, overflowing with daily fountains of tears and radiant with a twofold flame of charity, celebrated eucharist daily. After matins he proceeded alone to speak with the angels and then, immediately following, he plunged himself into cold water, remaining in it sufficiently long to subdue all the ardors of the flesh. The whole of the day he spent, inflexibly and unweariedly, in teaching, praying, genuflecting, and in care of the brethren. He also fed a multitude of orphans, wards, widows, needy, sick, feeble, and pilgrims. Thus he began; thus he continued; thus he ended his day. He imitated the monks of Egypt and lived a life like theirs.

Findbarr's Visit to David and David's Miraculous Horse

One time the most faithful abbot, Findbarr of Cork, became a pilgrim, yearning passionately to visit the shrines of St. Peter and

St. Paul, among others. When he had accomplished this, he turned back toward his own monastery, stopping off first to see David. There he stayed for some time in godly conversation with the holy man. His stay was further prolonged because the ship prepared for his return to his own country was held back by lack of wind. Afraid that the bond of charity would be weakened among the brethren in his absence, and that disputes, quarrels, and brawls would arise (just as bees, when their queen dies, pull apart and break up the honeycomb cells which they had fastened together with firmly binding wax), Findbarr anxiously searched for and found a wonderful way to return. He begged for David's horse, the one the holy man used to ride on church business. David granted him his request. Receiving the abbot's blessing, Findbarr reached the harbor and plunged into the sea, all the while putting his trust in David's blessing. Using the horse instead of a ship to carry him, he was taken through the towering waves as though on a level field.

As he travelled farther out into the sea, Findbarr came to where St. Brendan was leading a fabulous life on the back of a sea monster. When St. Brendan saw a man riding the sea on horseback, he cried in amazement, "Wonderful is God in his saints." The horseman approached so that they could exchange greetings. Then St. Brendan asked where he had come from, and how it was that he rode the sea on horseback. Findbarr told him of his pilgrimage and said, "Because my ship's delay was keeping me away from my brethren, the holy father Dewi presented me with his own horse, and thus fortified by his blessing, I ventured on such a road as this." "Go in peace," said Brendan to him, "I will come and see him."

Findbarr reached his country without mishap and told the brethren all that had happened to him. They kept the horse in the service of the monastery until its death, after which they made a statue in the shape of a horse to commemorate the miracle. Covered with gold, it remained on the island of Ireland and became famous for its many miracles.

David's Pilgrimage to Jerusalem

Dewi increased in holiness and in the esteem of good people. One night an angel appeared to him and said, "Tomorrow gird yourself and put on your sandals and set out to travel to

119

Jerusalem. This is the journey you have yearned to make. I will also summon two others to accompany you, Eliud and Paternus." But David, amazed at the authoritative command, asked in amazement, "How shall this be? For those whom you promise as companions are three or more days' journey from here and from each other. There is no way that we can come together by tomorrow." The angel said to him, "This very night I will go to each of them, and they will come to the meeting place I will now show you." Without delay David disposed of the contents of his cell and, with the blessings of the brethren, set forth in the early morning. When he reached the meeting place, he found the brethren there, according to the angel's promise, and together they began their journey. As fellow pilgrims they were equals; no one thought himself superior to another, and while each of them was servant, so each was master too. They prayed diligently, and with tears they watered their way. Their merits increased with every step they took. They truly had but one mind, one joy, one sorrow.

They sailed across the English Channel and came to Gaul, where they heard foreign languages spoken by different peoples. At length they approached the outskirts of Jerusalem, the city of their desire. The night before their arrival an angel appeared to the patriarch of Jerusalem in his sleep and said, "Three Christian men from the lands of the West are coming. Receive them with gladness and a hospitable welcome, and bless them and consecrate them bishops for me." The patriarch then prepared three thrones of the greatest distinction. When the saints reached the city, he rejoiced, and welcomed them warmly, and led them to the thrones prepared for them. Refreshed with godly conversation, they rendered thanks to God. Then, sustained by God's choices, the patriarch ordained David an archbishop. All things now completed, the three of them returned to their own land.

David's Last Days

Afterward, blessed and extolled by all, David was made archbishop of the entire British race by the unanimous consent of the bishops, kings, princes, nobles, and those of every rank. His city was also declared the metropolis of the whole country, so that whoever ruled it would be regarded as archbishop. Later, throughout all parts of the land the brethren built monasteries and churches. Everywhere voices were raised to heaven in prayer;

everywhere virtue existed; everywhere charitable offerings were distributed to the needy. The holy bishop Dewi was the supreme overseer, the supreme protector, the supreme preacher. From him all received their standard and pattern of living virtuously.

Eight days before the first day of March the brethren were keeping the hour of matins when an angel clearly spoke to David, "The day you have long desired is now close at hand." The holy bishop, recognizing the voice of a friend, rejoiced exceedingly and said to him, "Lord, take your servant in peace." His brethren, however, hearing only the sound and not being able to make out the words—for they had heard David and the angel conversing—fell to the ground in terror. Then the entire place was filled with angelic songs and fragrant perfumes. The holy bishop, with his mind fixed on heaven, cried with a loud voice, "Lord Jesus, receive my spirit." Then the angel spoke a second time, so that the brethren understood, "Prepare yourselves, for on the first day of March our Lord Jesus Christ, accompanied by a great host of angels, will come to meet you."

When the brothers heard this, they burst into tears. A profound sadness arose, and the city was filled with their weeping and with the words, "Holy bishop, take away our sorrow." David soothed and sustained them with consoling and comforting words, "Brothers, be steadfast, and bear to the end the yoke you have accepted." From that hour until the day of his death he remained in the church, preaching.

The report of this spread through the whole of Britain and Ireland, borne by an angel who said, "Do you know that in this coming week the holy bishop Dewi will depart to heaven?" Then, just like bees making for their hives on the approach of a storm, the assemblage of saints from both lands hastened to visit the holy father. The city overflowed with tears, the wailing echoing up to the stars, as young men mourned as if for a father and old men as if for a son. The following Sunday, in front of a vast multitude, David preached a most memorable sermon, and with undefiled hands, consecrated the Lord's body. Immediately after celebrating the eucharist he was seized with pains and became ill. He blessed the people and addressed them in these words: "Be joyful, brothers and sisters. Keep your faith and do the little things that you have seen and heard from me. On the third day, the first day of March, I shall go the way of my fathers. As for you, I say goodbye in the Lord's name." From that Sunday night until the fourth day after his death all who had come remained weeping, fasting, and keeping watch.

When the third day arrived, the place was filled with the most delightful fragrance, as well as choirs of angels singing melodiously. At the hour of matins, while the monks were singing hymns at divine service, our Lord Jesus Christ appeared for David's consolation, as the angel had promised. On seeing him, David was filled with joy and said, "Take me with you." With these words, and with Christ as his companion, he gave up his life to God. Then, attended by an escort of angels, David sought the portals of heaven. His body, borne on the arms of his brethren, was committed to the earth with all honor and was buried on the grounds of his own monastery. His soul, set free from the bonds of this transitory life, was crowned for all ages without end.

ETHNE & FEDELM
OF CONNACHT

Cruachain in Ireland was the site of the palace of the pagan kings of Connacht until Tara became the political capital. When Patrick was converting the island, King Loiguire's two beautiful young daughters lived there. As we know from Patrick's autobiographical *Confessio*, women were his primary supporters when he returned to Ireland as a missionary-bishop, and Ethne and Fedelm were evidently among his first converts. Little is known about them except the story that appears in the seventh-century hagiography by Tirechan, a monk from County Mayo. His account reveals that their druid mentors were also converted to the Christian faith. It also contains an ancient baptismal formula that was probably used in the Celtic churches. The questions the young women ask about God and Patrick's response to them surely rank as one of the most moving pieces of literature of the early Celtic church.

Ethne's and Fedelm's feast day is celebrated January 11. There is a wonderful stained-glass window portraying their conversion in the Catholic cathedral of Armagh. Contrary to modern beliefs, their deaths so soon after their baptism were not considered by Christian believers to be all that tragic. Certainly there was room for tears of grief, but in terms of eternity, union with God, not length of years, is the greatest reward any of us can receive. This is what the two women desired, and this is what they were given almost immediately.

At the Well Called Clebach

Patrick and his clerics went at sunrise to the well called Clebach on the slopes of Cruachain. Fair-haired Ethne and red-haired Fedelm, the daughters of Loiguire, son of Niall, went early, as they customarily did, to the well to wash. Beside the well the young women found the assembly of the clerics in white garments, with their books before them. They wondered at the shape of the clerics, and thought that they were men of other worlds or possibly apparitions. So they asked Patrick, "Who are you, and from where do you come?" Patrick said to them, "It would be better for you to believe in God than to inquire about our race." The elder daughter responded, "Who is your God, and where does he live? Tell us about him, how he is seen, how he is loved, how he is found. Tell us if he is youthful or very old; if he lives forever; if he is beautiful; if many people have fostered his son; if his daughters are recognized by men of the world as dear and beautiful."

Patrick, filled with the Holy Spirit, answered, "Our God is the God of all things, the God of heaven and earth and sea and river, the God of sun and moon and all the stars, the God of high mountains and lowly valleys, the God over heaven and in heaven and under heaven. He has a dwelling in heaven and earth and sea and all that dwell within them. He inspires all things; he gives life to all things; he surpasses all things. Our God kindles the light of the sun and the light of the moon. He made springs in arid land and dry islands in the sea; he appointed stars to minister to the greater lights. He has a Son coeternal with him and, like a son, very similar to his father. But the Son is not younger than the Father, nor is the Father older than the Son. And the Holy Spirit breathes in them. Father and Son and Holy Spirit are not divided. I desire to unite you to the Son of the heavenly king, for you are daughters of a king of earth."

The two young women said as if with one mouth and one heart, "How will we be able to believe in that king? Teach us so that we can see the Lord face to face. Teach us the way, and we will do whatever you tell us."

Patrick said to them, "Do you believe that through baptism you cast off the sins of your father and mother?" They answered, "We believe." "Do you believe in penance after sin?" "We believe."

"Do you believe in life after death, and in the resurrection on the last day?" "We believe." "Do you believe in the unity of the church?" "We believe," they replied. So they were baptized with a white garment over their heads. Then they demanded to see the face of Christ. Patrick said to them, "Unless you taste death and unless you receive the sacrament, you cannot see the face of Christ." They answered, "Give us the sacrament so that we may see the Son, our bridegroom." They received the eucharist of God and immediately fell asleep in death. Their friends placed them on one bed, covered them with their garments, and began to lament and keen greatly.

The druid Caplit, who had fostered the one daughter, came and wept, and Patrick preached to him and he believed. The hair of his head was shorn off. Then his brother Mael came and said, "My brother has believed Patrick, but I will not; instead I will bring him back to paganism." Then he spoke harsh words to Patrick. Patrick preached the faith to him and converted him to the penance of God, and his hair was shorn off, that is, the hair cut in the druid fashion. When the days of mourning for the king's daughters came to an end, the young women were buried by the well of Clebach, and Patrick blessed their remains.

FINDBARR of CORK

The Irish saint Findbarr, or Bairre, was founder of the monastery and city of Cork. He was born about 560, son of a master smith or craftsman who impregnated a royal slave girl. His parents settled with Findbarr in the region of Macroom where the new child was baptized. Findbarr studied under Bishop MacCuirb at Macroom. Another significant mentor was David of Wales, with whom he is said to have travelled to Rome. Findbarr preached in various parts of southern Ireland and lived for a time as a hermit on a small island called Gougane Barra. Although he founded other churches, his greatest accomplishment was the foundation of the monastery at Cork. This monastery attracted many disciples and its school became famous all over southern Ireland. In one of the stories about Findbarr and the *anamchara* ministry, we find a theological principle first enunciated by the desert fathers and mothers: even though a person may have different spiritual guides in his or her life, the ultimate *anamchara* or guide is the Holy Spirit.

The year of Findbarr's death has been variously calculated as 610, 623, 630, or 633. His cult in Ireland was based upon his teaching skills (he founded at least one monastic school, which included both female and male students) and his healing abilities. Findbarr died at Cloyne, and his body was taken for burial back to his church in Cork. This is now a magnificent cathedral. Today his island retreat at Gougane Barra is a popular pilgrimage site with a wooden cross marking the original place of Findbarr's hermitage and a small chapel with stained-glass windows telling the stories of other Irish saints. His feast day is September 25.

Findbarr's Illegitimate Conception and Amazing Birth

Findbarr's ancestors originated in Connacht, but settled in the district of Muscriage Mitine (west County Cork) where Amairgen, the father of Findbarr, owned land. Amairgen was a notable smith, in fact chief smith to Tigernach, the king of Rathlenn. There was a beautiful female slave in the house of this king, and Tigernach informed his entire household that none of them should have intercourse with her. Amairgen did not hear this, however. The smith and the young woman came together secretly, and their affair became known shortly thereafter when she conceived by him. After this King Tigernach summoned the woman and asked her by whom she was pregnant. She admitted truthfully that it was by Amairgen. Then the king ordered that they should both be bound, that a great fire be lit, and that the couple should be cast into it. However, because Findbarr was dear to God even before he was born, God did not allow the king to do this. He sent lightning and thunder and heavy rain so that they could not light the fire. Then the infant himself spoke from his mother's womb, and said: "O King, do not do this wicked deed, for it will not deepen your friendship with God." The king then said to his household, "Wait a while, so that we may see and know who is addressing us." Then the lightning and thunder and rain ceased, and Amairgen and the young woman were saved from being burned.

Soon after the woman gave birth to the wondrous boy, Findbarr. Immediately after his birth he addressed the king, telling him that his father and mother should be released to him. The king set them free at the child's request and surrendered himself and his posterity to Findbarr forever. After this the child did not speak again until the proper time.

His Fosterage by Three Clerics, and Name Change

Amairgen and the woman moved to Achad Durbcon, taking the little child with them. There the child was baptized by Bishop MacCuirb. The original name given to him was Loan. For seven years he was nurtured in his home.

There were three clerics of Munster who were on pilgrimage in Leinster at that time. On that journey they went to visit their own country. They came to the house of Amairgen and saw the beautiful little lad. The eldest of the three said: "Fair is that little boy, and the grace of the Holy Spirit shines in his face. It would be a pleasure for us to teach him." "If it be your pleasure," Amairgen responded, "take him with you, but wait until we return from a trip into Leinster."

The same three returned to the house of Amairgen in the summertime and took the boy with them. When they reached the hill called Muincille, the little boy became thirsty and cried, asking for a drink. The elder said to his servant: "Go to that doe there on the hill and bring from her a drink for the boy." The servant went and obtained a vessel full of milk from her, and it was given to the little boy. Then the elder said, "The place in which God wrought this wonderful miracle for the boy is a proper place for his instruction to begin, for his hair to be cut, and his name to be changed." And so it was done. The man who cut his hair said, "Beautiful and fair (*find*) is the crest (*barr*) on Loan." Added the elder, "You have spoken well. From now on this will be his name: Findbarr."

Findbarr's Love of Snow and His Becoming a Soul Friend at an Early Age

The three clerics mentioned above later came into the district of Leinster, and Findbarr accompanied them. He marked out the church of Mac Cathail in Gowran Pass, and there Findbarr read his psalms. Once, while Findbarr was reading his psalms, a heavy snowstorm left a hood of snow around the cell in which he was studying his lessons. Findbarr said to his tutor, Lochan, "I would like this hood to remain around my cell until I have finished my psalms." God heard his prayer, for the snow melted from the earth, but the snow around Findbarr's cell remained until he had finished his psalms.

Once a certain rich man, Fidach by name, arrived at Findbarr's cell in order to ask Lochan to be his soul friend. Lochan said to Fidach, "Kneel to that little lad there, to Findbarr." Fidach resisted his command, saying, "I think it is insulting to kneel before a young boy." Lochan then told Fidach, "If I take Findbarr as my soul friend, will you do the same?" Fidach said he would. Then the two of them knelt before Findbarr, and Lochan offered his church to God and to Findbarr, while Fidach offered himself and his descendants to him. Findbarr told his tutor, "Receive this man and his descendants from me in return for teaching me my psalms."

His Miracles and the Request of His Mentor

Findbarr went to Bishop MacCuirb. This MacCuirb was a well-known man, a fellow pupil of David of Cell Muine. Both of them had been pupils of Gregory of Rome. When Findbarr came to Bishop MacCuirb, the king, Fachtna Fergach the Elder, addressed him, saying, "I want you to bless my two children, my blind son and my mute daughter." Findbarr blessed them both and they were healed; the son could see again, and the daughter could speak. As they were conversing together, Findbarr and the king heard a great lamentation. "What is that?" asked Findbarr. The king replied, "I believe my wife has just died!" Findbarr said to him, "God is able to raise her from the dead." After this the saint blessed water, and they washed the queen with it. She arose from death, as if she were rising from sleep. As the two men resumed their conversation, the king asked him, "Can you, Findbarr, perform any other miracles in my presence?" Findbarr replied, "God is able to do them, if God pleases." Just then, even though it was spring, ripe nuts fell from a hazel tree under which they were standing, so that from their feet up to their chests they were covered with them.

After this Findbarr studied the Book of Matthew and the Acts of the Apostles with Bishop MacCuirb. When the bishop demanded a stipend for his instruction, Findbarr asked, "What fee do you demand?" Bishop MacCuirb replied, "This is my wish: that the resurrection of us both may be in the same place on the Day of Judgment." Findbarr responded, "You will have your wish, for you will be buried in the same place as I am, and we will have our resurrection together."

Findbarr's School for Men and Women, and His Travels

Findbarr lived on Loch Iree, in Edergole to the east of the lake. This was the school he started. Eolang was the tutor, and the male students were Colman, Baichine, Nesan, Garban, Talmach, and others. All these offered their churches to God and to Findbarr in perpetuity. With him in Edergole were numerous women, including Findbarr's own sister, who also offered their churches to God and to Findbarr.

Some time later, with an angel guiding him, Findbarr came to his own district and built a church. A cave is located there called Cuas Barrai (Findbarr's Cave). Nearby is a beautiful pool in which every night Findbarr caught a salmon in his net. The angel said to him, however, "This will not be your place of resurrection." So Findbarr crossed the river to Cell na Cluaine (Gougane Barra) where he built a church and remained for some time. Two pupils of Ruadan, Cormac and Buichin, came to him there. They had asked Ruadan where they should go, and Ruadan had said to them, "Go with my blessing, and the place where your bell rings and the strap of your book-wallet breaks, that will be your place of resurrection." When they came to Findbarr at Cell na Cluaine, all those things happened to them as Ruadan had predicted. They were depressed, however, thinking that the church would not be given to them, but Findbarr assured them, "Do not be sad or depressed. I give this church and all its treasures to you and to God."

Findbarr built twelve churches before he came to Cork, and he gave them all up out of humility and the greatness of his charity.

He Finds His Place of Resurrection

The angel guided Findbarr from Cell na Cluaine to the place where Cork stands today and said to him, "Stay here, for here will be your place of resurrection." Findbarr then fasted for three days, until Aed, son of Comgall, came to him. Aed was seeking a cow that had wandered away to give birth to her calf, and he found her with three clerics. Aed asked, "What has brought you here?" Findbarr answered, "We are seeking a place where we can pray to God for ourselves and for the man who will give it to us." Aed said, "I give you this place and the cow by which God has led you there."

After this the angel of God asked, "Do you wish to remain here?" Findbarr replied, "Yes, if it is God's will." The angel told him, "If you remain here, fewer sons and daughters of life will go to heaven from here. Go a little further east to where there are many waters and remain there on the advice of the Lord. Many will be the sages and children of life of that place who will go to heaven." The angel then led him to the place designated by God, and the angel marked out the church and blessed it. Findbarr remained there.

His Pilgrimage to Rome and Consecration as Bishop

Findbarr, together with Eolang, Maedoc of Ferns, and David of Cell Muine, accompanied by twelve other monks, went to Rome to receive episcopal orders. Gregory was successor of St. Peter at that time. When Gregory raised his hand over Findbarr's head to consecrate him, a flame suddenly came down from heaven and hit his hand. Gregory said to Findbarr, "Go home, and the Lord himself will read the episcopal orders over you." And that is how it happened.

When Findbarr arrived at his own church, the Lord himself read the order over him at the cross in front of the church where his remains were later buried. Oil flowed abundantly out of the earth there, so that it rose up over his sandals and over the sandals of the elders who were with him. That oil healed every ailment to which it was later applied. Then Findbarr and his elders blessed the church and the cemetery, praying that there would be an abundance of wisdom in Cork forever.

After this Findbarr remained in Cork and had with him a great school of saints, many of whom later became bishops and offered their churches to God and to Findbarr.

Bishop MacCuirb said to Findbarr: "If my body is the first to be buried here, and my soul goes straight to heaven, I will not allow anyone who dies and is buried in this cemetery to go to hell." The corpse of Bishop MacCuirb was the first to be buried in the soil of Cork.

Findbarr's Search for a Soul Friend

After the death of Bishop MacCuirb, Findbarr was much concerned at being without a soul friend. So he went to visit Eolang, and God revealed to Eolang that Findbarr was coming to see him. Eolang said to his monastic family, "Noble guests will come to us today, and you must hospitably feed and bathe them." Soon Findbarr arrived, and Eolang's guestmaster met him, welcomed him, and said, "Eolang is aware of your arrival. Please let me take your clothes, so that you and your attendants can bathe yourselves." Findbarr replied, "We would first like to see Eolang."

The guestmaster went to confer with his master and told him of Findbarr's response. Eolang said: "Let Findbarr bathe first, and we will converse later. Let him go to his monastery tomorrow, and I will come to him at the end of the week."

Eolang came to Cork as he had promised at the end of the week. He immediately knelt before Findbarr and said the following, "I offer to you my church, my body, and my soul." Findbarr wept openly and said, "This was not my thought, but that it would be I who would offer my church to you." Eolang said, "Let it be as I have said, for this is the will of God. You are dear to God, and you are greater than myself. One thing only I ask, that our resurrection will be in the same place." Findbarr replied, "Your wish will be fulfilled, but I am still troubled about the soul friendship." Eolang told him, "You shall receive today a soul friend worthy of yourself." This was done as he said, for Eolang in the presence of the angels and archangels placed Findbarr's hand in the hand of the Lord himself and said, "O Lord, take this just man to yourself." Then the Lord took the hand of Findbarr and began leading him to heaven. But Eolang cried out, "O Lord, do not take Findbarr from me now, but wait until the time of his death when the soul leaves the body." The Lord then released Findbarr's hand, and from that day no one could look upon his hand because of its radiance. Because of this he wore a glove on his hand continuously.

A Litany of Praise to Findbarr

The miracles and mighty works God wrought for St. Findbarr are too numerous to recount. No one would be able to narrate them all unless God himself or an angel of God should come to relate them. Still, some mention of them may suffice as an illustration of Findbarr's inner life and his daily conversation, his humility, his obedience, his compassion, his sweetness, his patience and gentleness, his love and pity and readiness to forgive, his fasting and abstinence, his earnest prayer, his patient waiting, and his heart continually set on God.

Findbarr was a just man with the transparency of a patriarch, a true pilgrim like Abraham. He was compassionate, simple, and forgiving of heart like Moses. He was a laudable and gifted psalmist like David. He was a treasury of wisdom and knowledge like Solomon, the son of David. Like Paul the apostle, he was a chosen vessel of righteousness; like the youthful John, he was a man full of the grace and favor of the Holy Spirit.

Findbarr was a lion of strength and power; he was a serpent of cunning and wisdom in everything good; he was a dove in gentleness and simplicity in the face of all evil. He was a fair garden full of herbs of virtue. He was the crystal fountain through whose teaching the sins of the people whom God entrusted to him were washed away. He was also a heavenly cloud, a golden lamp lighted by the Holy Spirit, a shining fire with heat to warm and kindle love in the hearts of the children of life. He was the precious stone with which the heavenly palace was adorned; the crystal vessel in which the wine of the word of God was distributed; the rich and prosperous husbandman of wisdom and knowledge who paid the righteous poor with the abundance of his teaching. He was a branch of the true vine, Christ, sent to satisfy and bring life to the world. He was the true leech who healed sicknesses and diseases of the body and soul of every believer in the church.

Findbarr's Death

After healing the blind and the leper, the lame, the deaf and the dumb, and other sick folk of every kind; after founding many churches and cells and monasteries for God; after ordaining many bishops, priests, and people of every other rank for baptism, confirmation, communion, confession, instruction, and the maintenance of the faith in those districts, Findbarr went to Cell na Cluaine (Gougane Barra) to visit Cormac and Baithine. Fiama also went to meet him at Cell na Cluaine, and they blessed each other as holy brothers. Findbarr said to them all, "It is time for me to be released from the prison of the body and to go to the heavenly king who is calling me now." After this, Findbarr took the eucharist from the hand of Fiama, and by the cross in the middle of Cell na Cluaine sent forth his spirit to heaven. His monks and disciples and the synod of the churches of Desmond later came to wake and honor the body of their master, St. Findbarr, and to bear it with them to the place of his resurrection, Cork.

This day—the day of Findbarr's death—was prolonged for the elders. God did not allow the sun to go beneath the earth for twelve days afterward. That was as long as the synod of the churches of Desmond were busy preparing the body of their master with hymns and psalms, with Masses and recitation of the hours. Then the angels of heaven came to meet his soul and carried it with them with honor and reverence to heaven where he shines like the sun in the company of the patriarchs and prophets, in the company of the apostles and disciples of Jesus, in the company of the nine heavenly orders of angels who sinned not, in the company of the divinity and the humanity of the Son of God, in the company that is higher than any company, the company of the Holy Trinity, Father, Son, and Holy Spirit.

HILD
OF WHITBY

ild of Whitby, one of the great woman soul friends of Northumbria, was born in 614. Although Anglo-Saxon, she was a protégée of Aidan of Lindisfarne, who encouraged her to found a number of monasteries in northern England, including the double monastery at Whitby. The monastic school established there became known for its fine education of students, at least five of whom later became bishops. It was also the home of the first English poet, Caedmon, whose vocation as a writer was affirmed by Hild.

Her reputation as a talented abbess and much-sought-after spiritual guide certainly contributed to King Oswy's choice of Whitby as the place to hold a council or synod in 664. This meeting was called to decide questions in dispute between the Celtic and Roman parties in the Northumbrian church related to the dating of Easter, the tonsure, and other less explicit aspects of church governance and spirituality. As Bede the Venerable makes clear, Hild was definitely on the side of the Irish and their followers.

Bede tells us that Hild was a challenging director who was not afraid of pushing those who sought her out or whom she ruled as abbess. Hers was evidently the type of challenge, however, that did not alienate. Bede states clearly that "all who knew her called her mother"—a term of endearment that was commonly used among the desert Christians for wise and holy female guides. Hild had a great variety of competencies. She was not only able to administer well a large double monastery, but was also adept at one-to-one guidance, as is clear by the number of royalty and common folk who sought her out. It is interesting to note the virtues Bede associated with her leadership and the order in which he lists them: justice, devotion, chastity, peace, and love.

Hild died in the autumn of 680 after seven years of a painfully lingering illness (probably tuberculosis). Besides the medieval monastic ruins that today mark the spot of her original monastery at Whitby, there is a wonderful carving of her on a modern high cross overlooking the churning waves of the North Sea. Hild's feast day is celebrated November 17.

Hild's Life and Career

Hild, abbess at the monastery of Whitby and a most devoted servant of Christ, died on November 17 in the year of our Lord 680. She was sixty-six. After accomplishing many heavenly deeds on earth, she departed this world to receive the rewards of heaven. Her career falls into two equal parts: she spent her first thirty-three years very nobly in the secular habit, then she dedicated an equal number of years still more nobly to the Lord in the monastic life. Hild was of noble birth, the daughter of Hereric, King Edwin's nephew. With Edwin she received the faith and the mysteries of Christ through the teaching of Paulinus, the first bishop of the Northumbrians. She preserved that faith undefiled until she was counted worthy to see God.

When Hild decided to give up the secular habit and serve only the Lord, she withdrew to the kingdom of the East Angles, for she was related to a king of that land. Her desire was to leave her home and all that she had, and cross over, if possible, to Gaul in order to live as a stranger for the Lord's sake in the monastery of Chelles. Thus she hoped to more easily obtain her eternal home in heaven.

At that time her sister Hereswith, mother of Ealdwulf, king of the East Angles, was living in the monastery under the discipline of the rule and awaiting her heavenly reward. Hild, inspired by her sister's example, continued to live for a year in the kingdom of the East Angles with the intention of going abroad. Then Bishop Aidan called her home, and she received a hide of land on the north side of the river Wear. There she lived the monastic life with a small band of companions for another year.

Hild as Abbess and Counselor

After this Hild was made abbess in the monastery called Heruteu (Hartlepool). This monastery had been established shortly before by Heiu, a devout handmaid of Christ, who is said to have been the first woman in the Northumbrian kingdom to take the vows and habit of a nun. Heiu was consecrated by Bishop Aidan. Soon after she founded the monastery, however, Heiu retired to the town of Calcaria, which the English call Koelcacoestir, where she made her home. Hild, the handmaiden of Christ, was appointed to rule the monastery. She immediately set about establishing there a rule of life which in many ways was similar to that which she had learned from certain wisdom figures. Bishop Aidan and others who knew her visited her often, instructed her assiduously, and loved her with all of their hearts because of her own innate wisdom and her dedication to the service of God.

When she had ruled over the monastery for some years, entirely occupied with establishing a rule of life there, she decided to either found or to set in order a monastery at a place called Streanoeshalch (Whitby), a task, though imposed upon her, which she carried out with great enthusiasm. She established there the same rule of life as in the other monastery and taught the community to observe strictly the virtues of justice, devotion, chastity, and other virtues. Above all, she wanted her monastic community to continue in peace and charity. Like the primitive church, no one at that monastery was rich, and no one was in need, for they had all things in common and none had any private possessions. So great was Hild's prudence that ordinary people as well as kings and princes sought and received her advice when they were facing difficulties. She encouraged those under her direction to devote a certain amount of time to the study of the holy scriptures and to the performance of good works.

The Dream of Hild's Mother and Hild's Works of Light

All who knew Hild used to call her mother because of her outstanding devotion and grace. She was not only a model of the holy life to all who lived in the monastery, but she also provided an opportunity for salvation and repentance to many who lived far away and heard the story of her diligence and virtue. This had to happen in fulfillment of a dream her mother, Breguswith, had during the child's infancy.

While her husband Hereric was living in exile under the British king Cerdic, where he was eventually poisoned, Breguswith had a dream that her husband was suddenly taken away and, though she searched for him everywhere, no trace of him could be found. Suddenly, in the midst of her search, Breguswith found a valuable necklace under her garment, and as she gazed upon it intently, it seemed to spread such a blaze of light that it filled all Britain with its gracious splendor. This dream was fulfilled in her daughter Hild, for her life was an example of the works of light.

The Easter Controversy and the Council of Whitby

When Bishop Aidan died, a great controversy arose over the celebration of Easter. Those who had come from Kent or Gaul stated that the Irish observance of Easter Sunday was contrary to the custom of the universal church. One of the most passionate defenders of the true Easter was Ronan, who, although Irish by race, had learned the true rules of the church in Gaul or Italy. [Bede agrees strongly with the Roman party on this matter.] In arguing with Finan, Aidan's successor at Lindisfarne, Ronan set many right or at least encouraged them to search more diligently for the truth. He, however, could not get Finan to agree. On the contrary, as he was a man of violent temper, Ronan made Finan the more bitter by his reproofs and, indeed, turned him into an open adversary of the truth. James, once the deacon of the venerable Archbishop Paulinus, kept the true and catholic Easter with all those whom he could instruct in the better way. Queen Eanflaed and her people also observed Easter as she had seen it done in Kent, having with her a Kentish priest named Romanus who also followed the Catholic observance. Thus it is said that in those days Easter was sometimes celebrated twice in the same year, so that when the king had finished the fast and was observing Easter Sunday, the queen and her people were still in Lent and observing Palm Sunday. This difference in the celebration of Easter was tolerated patiently by all while Aidan, who followed the Celtic practice, was alive, because the people clearly understood that he could not keep Easter other than according to the custom of those who had sent him. However, when Finan, Aidan's successor, died and Colman, who had also been sent from Ireland, became bishop, conflict over this question of Easter, the tonsure, and other ecclesiastical matters became heated. It was decided to hold a council to settle the dispute at the monastery called Streanoeshealh (Whitby), a name that means "the bay of the lighthouse." The devout woman Hild was abbess there.

The Deliberations at Whitby and King Oswy's Decision

Two kings came to the council, father and son Oswy and Alhfrith, as well as Bishop Colman with his Irish clergy, and Agilbert with the priests Agatho and Wilfrid. James and Romanus were on their side, while the Abbess Hild and her followers were on the side of the Irish. The venerable Bishop Cedd also came. He had been consecrated long before by the Irish and acted as a most careful interpreter for both parties at the council.

King Oswy began by declaring that it seemed fitting that those who served one God should observe one rule of life and not differ in the celebration of the heavenly sacraments, since they all hoped for one kingdom in heaven. Therefore, he said, they ought to determine the truer tradition and then all follow it together. He ordered Bishop Colman to explain the customs he followed and their origins. Colman responded: "The method of keeping Easter I observe I received from my superiors, who sent me here as a bishop. It was the way that all our elders, men beloved of God, are said to have celebrated it. This method is neither contemptible nor blameworthy, since we believe the blessed evangelist John, the disciple whom the Lord especially loved, celebrated it in this way, together with all the churches over which he presided." After Colman had explained all this and more to the same effect, the king ordered Agilbert to explain the method he observed, its origin, and the authority he had for following it. Agilbert answered, "I ask that my disciple, the priest Wilfrid, speak on my behalf, for we both agree with the other followers of our church tradition who are present. He can explain our views in the English tongue better and more clearly than I can through an interpreter." Wilfrid, receiving permission from the king to speak, began in this way: "The Easter we celebrate is the same as that universally celebrated in Rome, where the apostles St. Peter and St. Paul lived, taught, suffered, and were buried. We have found it in use everywhere in Italy and Gaul when we travelled through those countries for the purpose of study and prayers. We have also

141

learned that it is observed in the same way in Africa, Asia, Egypt, Greece, and throughout the whole world, wherever the church of Christ is scattered, among various nations and languages. The only exceptions are these men and their stubborn accomplices—I mean the Picts and the Britons—who in these, the two remotest islands of the ocean and only in some parts of them, foolishly attempt to fight against the whole world."

The argument continued between Colman and Wilfrid—with Colman finally stating that he and the Irish were following the example of Columcille from Iona and his followers, "men beloved of God." Wilfrid condescendingly responded:

"Though your fathers were holy men, do you think that a handful of people in one corner of the remotest of islands is to be preferred to the universal church of Christ, which is spread throughout the world? Even if that Columcille of yours—yes, and ours too, if he belonged to Christ—was a holy man of mighty works, is he to be preferred to the most holy chief of the apostles, to whom the Lord said, 'You are Peter and upon this rock I will build my church and the gates of hell shall not prevail against it, and I will give to you the keys of the kingdom of heaven'?"

After Wilfrid had finished, the king asked, "Is it true, Colman, that the Lord said these words to Peter?" Colman answered, "King, it is true." Then the king asked another question: "Have you anything to show that an equal authority was given to your Columcille?" Colman answered, "Nothing." Again the king said, "Do you both agree, then, that these words were addressed primarily to Peter and that the Lord gave him the keys of the kingdom of heaven?" Both men replied, "Yes." Thereupon the king concluded, "Then, I tell you, since Peter is the doorkeeper, I will not contradict him; I intend to obey his commands to the best of my knowledge and ability in everything. Otherwise when I arrive at the gates of the kingdom of heaven, there may be no one to open them because the one who in your own estimation holds the keys has turned his back on me." When the king had spoken, all who were seated there or standing nearby, both high and low, signified their agreement. They gave up their imperfect rules and readily accepted those that they recognized to be better.

Once the dispute was ended and the assembly had disbanded, Colman understood that his teachings had been rejected and that his principles were despised. He then took those who wanted to follow him, that is, those who would not accept the Catholic Easter and the tonsure in the shape of the crown—for there was a great argument about that too—and returned to Ireland.

Hild Helps the Poet Caedmon Discover His Vocation

In Hild's monastery there was a certain brother who was especially close to God and who used to compose holy and religious songs. Whatever he learned from the holy scriptures through interpreters, he quickly turned into delightful and moving poetry in English, which was his native tongue. Through his songs many were inspired to despise the world and to yearn for the heavenly life. Although it is true that after him other Englishmen attempted to compose religious poems, none could compare with him, for he did not learn the art of poetry from any group or individual, but freely received the gift of song by the grace of God. Thus this man could never compose any foolish or trivial poem, but only those concerned with spirituality. He had lived as a layman until he was quite mature in years, but had never learned any songs. Sometimes, in fact, at a feast, when everyone took a turn singing, this man would get up when he saw the harp approach, go out, and return home.

One time he left the place of feasting and went to the cattle barn, since it was his turn to be in charge of them that night. Soon he stretched himself out and went to sleep. He dreamed that someone stood by him, greeted him, and called him by name: "Caedmon," the dream figure said, "sing me something." Caedmon answered, "I cannot sing. That is why I left the feast and came here." Again the speaker said, "Nevertheless, you must sing to me." "What must I sing?" asked Caedmon. The dream figure said, "Sing about the beginning of creation." Caedmon began to sing verses he had never heard before in praise of God the Creator. This is the general sense of what he sang: "Let us praise the Creator of the heavenly kingdom, the power of the Creator and his counsel, the deeds of the Father of glory; how he, since he is the eternal God, was the author of all marvels and first created the heavens as a roof for the human race and then, as the almighty Guardian of humankind, created the earth." This is the sense but not the exact content of what Caedmon sang as he slept, for it is impossible to translate verses, however well composed, from one language to another without some loss of beauty and dignity. When

143

Caedmon awoke, he remembered all that he had sung while asleep. Soon he added more verses in the same manner, praising God in a suitable way.

The next morning Caedmon went to his master and told him of the gift he had received. The man took him to Abbess Hild. He was then told to describe his dream to a number of the more learned men, and also to recite his song so that they might all examine him and discern the nature and origin of the gift. It seemed apparent to all of them that the Lord had granted him heavenly grace. They then read to him a passage of sacred history or doctrine, telling him make a song out of it, if he could, in metrical form. Caedmon accepted the task and left. When he returned the next morning, he repeated the passage he had been given, which he had put into excellent verse.

Abbess Hild, recognizing the grace the man had received, instructed him to renounce his secular habit and to take monastic vows. She and all her people received him into the community and ordered him to be instructed in the whole course of sacred history. Caedmon learned all that he could by listening to his teachers. Then, memorizing it and ruminating over it, like some clean animal chewing the cud, he turned it into the most melodious verse. As he recited it, it sounded so sweet that his teachers in turn became his audience. Caedmon sang about the creation of the world, the origin of the human race, and the whole history of Genesis, of the departure of Israel from Egypt, the entry into the promised land, and of many other stories taken from the sacred scriptures. He sang of the incarnation, passion, and resurrection of the Lord, of his ascension into heaven, of the coming of the Holy Spirit, and the teaching of the apostles. He also composed songs about the terrors of future judgment, the horrors of the pains of hell, and the joys of the heavenly kingdom, as well as many other songs about God's mercies and judgments. In all of them he attempted to turn his hearers away from the delight of sin and arouse in them the love and practice of good works.

Hild's Lingering Sickness and Death

When Hild had administered her monastery for many years, the blessed Author of our salvation subjected her holy soul to a long physical illness so that, like the apostle Paul, her strength might be made perfect in weakness. She was attacked by a fever, which tortured her with its burning heat, and for six years she suffered continually from that sickness. During all this time, however, she never stopped giving thanks to her Maker and to instruct publicly and privately the flock committed to her charge. Taught by her own experience, she admonished them all, when health of body was given to them, to serve the Lord dutifully and, when in adversity or sickness, always to return thanks to the Lord faithfully. In the seventh year of her illness Hild began to suffer internal pain and her last day arrived. About cock-crow she received the viaticum of the most holy eucharist and then summoned the handmaidens of Christ who were in the monastery. She urged them to preserve the gospel peace among themselves and toward all others. While still exhorting them, she joyfully saw death approach or rather, to use the words of the Lord, she "passed from death into life."

The same night and in the same monastery in which this servant of God died, her death was seen in a vision by one of the devoted virgins of God who loved her dearly. This woman saw Hild's soul ascend to heaven in the company of angels. She told the servants of Christ who were with her about it at the time it happened and encouraged them to pray for Hild's soul. This happened even before the rest of the community knew of Hild's death, for people were only informed of it when they met the next morning. This nun was at the time with one other handmaiden of Christ in the remotest part of the monastery, where the women who had recently entered the monastic life used to spend their novitiate until they were fully instructed and admitted into the fellowship of the community.

IA
OF CORNWALL

Ia, or Hya, is the patron of the picturesque town of St. Ives in Cornwall, which is located in southwestern England. According to local tradition she was a religious woman of noble birth who came to Cornwall as a missionary from Ireland in the fifth or sixth century with the monks Gwinear, Fingar, and Piala. She was said to be the sister of Euny, and to have journeyed later to Brittany with 777 disciples. She was martyred there. The *Life of St. Gwinear*, written about 1300 by Anselm, a monk living in Brittany, relates how Gwinear and his companions, on leaving Ireland for Cornwall, left Ia behind on the beach. The story that follows once again demonstrates the persistence and faith of Irish women, and in particular, Ia's trust in God to provide.

St. Ives parish church in Cornwall is located near the harbor. It has a medieval stone baptismal fount, a beautiful Lady's Chapel, and marvelous paintings and wood carvings of the Celtic saints. Considering the number of towns in Cornwall named after the saints, a popular saying rings true: There are more saints in Cornwall than there are in heaven. St. Ia's feast day is February 3.

Ia's Prayer and the Miraculous Leaf

Gwinear and his companions left Ireland for Cornwall. They had not gone far when a virgin of noble birth, named Ia, came down to the shore intent upon going with them. When she discovered that she was too late, she was filled with grief and knelt down on the beach to pray. As she did so, she noticed a little leaf floating on the water. Ia touched it with the rod she carried to see if it would sink. Lo! it began to grow larger and larger as she looked at it. Believing that it was sent to her by God, and trusting in him, she embarked upon the leaf and was immediately wafted across the Channel, reaching her destination before the others.

ITA

OF KILLEEDY

Ita (also Ite or Ide) is, after Brigit, the most famous of Irish women soul friends. Her hagiographer even describes her as "a second Brigit." A sixth-century abbess, Ita founded a monastery in County Limerick at Killeedy (which means Cell or Church of Ita). She came from the highly respected clan of the Deisi, and her father, like Brigit's, was resistant to her becoming a nun. After gaining his permission, Ita left home and settled at the foot of Sliabh Luachra, where other women from neighboring clans soon joined her. There she founded a monastic school for the education of small boys, one of whom was Brendan of Clonfert. She evidently had many students, for she is called the "foster-mother of the saints of Erin."

Ita's original name, some claim, was Deirdre, but because of her thirst (*iota*) for holiness she became known as Ita. This quality may have been what drew so many women to join her monastery and families to send their sons to her. Ita wanted her students to become acquainted with the saints as soul friends. Besides her mentoring, Ita is associated with competence in healing and with an asceticism that an angel had to warn her about. This story seems to be saying that while fasting can be important, it should not be taken to an extreme. She is portrayed in the following stories as a powerful female confessor who is not afraid of giving penances, and yet who is at the same time especially forgiving and compassionate.

Ita died in approximately 570. Her grave, frequently decorated with flowers, is in the ruins of a Romanesque church at Killeedy where her monastery once stood. A holy well nearby, almost invisible now, was known for centuries for curing smallpox in children and other diseases as well. Her feast day is January 15.

Ita's Qualities as a Child, and the Fiery Grace of God

Ita was born in Ireland of noble lineage, that is, of the stock of Feidhlimidh Reachtmiher, by whom all Ireland was supremely ruled for many years from the royal fort of Tara. He had three sons, Fiacha, Cond, and Eochaid. Ita was born of the people called the Deisi, and from her baptism on she was filled with the Holy Spirit. All marvelled at her childhood purity and behavior, and her abstinence on the days she had to fast. She performed many miracles while she was yet a small child, and when she could speak and walk she was prudent, very generous and mild toward everyone, gentle and chaste in her language, and God-fearing. She consistently attempted to overcome evil and always did what she could to promote good. As a young girl she lived at home with her parents.

One day while Ita was asleep in her room the whole place seemed to be on fire. When her neighbors came to give assistance, however, the fire in her room seemed to have been extinguished. All marvelled at that, and it was said that it was the grace of God that blazed about Ita as she slept. When she arose from her sleep, her whole appearance seemed to be angelic, for she had beauty that has never been seen before or since. Her appearance was such that her friends could hardly gaze upon her, and so all recognized that it was the grace of God that burned about her. After a short interval her original appearance returned, which certainly was beautiful enough.

Ita's Dream and the Angel That Helped Discern Its Meaning

Another day when she went to sleep, Ita saw an angel of the Lord approach her and give her three precious stones. When she awoke she did not know what that dream signified, and she had a question in her heart about it. Then an angel appeared to her and said, "Why are you wondering about that dream? Those three precious stones you saw being given to you signify the coming of the Blessed Trinity to you, Father, Son, and Holy Spirit. Always in your sleep and vigils the angels of God and holy visions will come to you, for you are a temple of God, in body and soul." After saying this, the angel left her.

Ita's Desire to be Consecrated to Christ, and Her Parents' Resistance

Another day Ita came to her mother and announced to her the divine precepts the Holy Spirit had taught her. She asked her mother to seek her father's permission so that she might consecrate herself to Christ. But her father was defiantly opposed to what she desired. The request was also very displeasing to her mother, and when others added their petitions, Ita's father vehemently refused to give permission. Then Ita, filled with the spirit of prophecy, said to all: "Leave my father alone for a while. Though he now forbids me to be consecrated to Christ, he will come to persuade me and eventually will order me to do so, for he will be compelled by Jesus Christ my Lord to let me go wherever I wish to serve God." And it happened as she had predicted. This is how it came about.

Not long afterward, Ita fasted for three days and three nights. During those days and nights, through dreams and vigils, it became clear that the devil was waging several battles against Ita. She, however, resisted him in everything, whether she slept or watched. One night the devil, sad and grieving, left Ita with these words: "Alas, Ita, you will free yourself from me, and many others too will be delivered." That very night an angel of the Lord came to Ita's father and said: "Why do you forbid your daughter to accept the veil of virginity in Christ's name? For she will be a great and famous virgin before God and his saints and will be the protector of many on the Day of Judgment. You will not only allow her to accept the sign of virginity, but you will let her go wherever she wants in order to serve Christ. She will serve God in another people, and she will be the mother of that people." Hearing this, Ita's father came to her immediately and told her all that he had heard. As the virgin had foretold, he gave her his permission to leave, and also urged her to take the veil of virginity and to go wherever she wished. That very day, having completed the three-day fast, Ita went to the church to receive the veil.

151

Ita Finds a Place for Her Monastery

As Ita was journeying, a great crowd of demons approached her and began to attack her fiercely. The angels of God descended from the heavens and fought strongly with the demons on Ita's behalf. Overcome by the angels the demons fled in all directions crying out and saying, "Woe to us, for from this day on we will not be able to fight against this virgin." In the meantime, Ita, consoled by the angels, came to a church where she was consecrated by the clerics at the angels' command and received the veil of virginity.

Then Ita prayed to the Lord to show her the place where she should serve him. An angel of the Lord came to her and said: "Leave your native district and come to the area called Ui Conaill and remain in the western part of it, near the foot of Sliabh Luachra. There the angel of the Lord will come to you and will show you the place where your convent will be. You will be the patron of the people of Ui Conaill; God has granted that people to you and to St. Senan." When Ita heard these words from the angel, she went with her companions to that region and remained at the foot of Sliabh Luachra, as the angel had told her. The angel came to her immediately and assigned her the place where she would serve God.

From there the fame of Ita travelled throughout the entire region. Many virgins came to her from different places to serve God under her care. She received them all piously and cheerfully. Having heard of her great holiness, the people of Ui Conaill came with their chieftain and wanted to donate all the land around her cell to her and to God in perpetuity. Ita, however, did not wish to be involved in worldly concerns, and she accepted only four acres as a vegetable garden. The chieftain and his followers were very displeased by that and they said, "What you do not wish to accept now, when you go to God's kingdom, will be bestowed upon you." And so it happened. All the people of Ui Conaill took Ita as their patron from then on, as the angel had foretold. Ita blessed that people and their land with many blessings. They all returned home with great joy, and it became their custom to bring many gifts and alms to the monastery in honor of St. Ita for the use of the holy virgins.

An Angel Warns Her About Her Excessive Fasting

Ita fasted for two or three successive days, and often for four days. Then an angel of the Lord came to her one day when she was worn out with hunger and said, "You are afflicting your body with too much fasting; you should not do so." But Ita did not wish to lighten her burden, so the angel added: "God has given you this grace: From this day until your death, you will be refreshed by heavenly food. You will not be able to refuse to eat when the angel of the Lord comes to you with a meal." Then Ita, bowing down to the ground, thanked God, and she shared the meal with others whom she considered worthy to receive it. And so Ita lived on the heavenly food brought to her by the angel until her death.

Ita's Advice to a Holy Nun

One day a holy nun came to Ita and spoke to her about the divine commandments. When they were conversing together, that virgin said to Ita: "In God's name, tell us why you are loved more by God than any other virgin we know of in the world. We know that food from heaven is given to you by God; that you heal all illnesses by your prayers; that you prophesy about things past and to come; that the demons everywhere flee from you; that angels of the Lord speak to you daily; and that you persevere unhindered in meditation and prayer to the blessed Trinity."

Ita replied: "You have answered your own question when you say, 'you persevere unhindered in meditation and prayer to the blessed Trinity.' If anyone acts in that way, God will be ever with that person; if I have done so from my infancy, then all those things you have said did happen to me." After hearing Ita's words concerning prayer and meditation on God, that holy nun went back rejoicing to her convent.

Ita's Effectiveness as a Confessor

A nun who had been under Ita's charge committed fornication. On the following day, Ita summoned her and said: "Why did you not care, sister, to guard your virginity?" The nun, however, denied that she had committed fornication. Ita said to her: "Did you really not commit fornication yesterday in such-and-such a place?" The nun saw immediately that Ita could prophesy about things past and present. She admitted the truth and was healed, doing penance according to Ita's command.

Another virgin, living far away from Ita in the province of Connacht, secretly committed adultery. Full of the spirit of prophecy, Ita knew this, and ordered St. Brendan to bring the nun to her. St. Brendan made the woman go to Ita. Ita then described to her, among other things, how she had conceived and given birth to a son. When the woman heard her sin from Ita's mouth, she made a fitting penance. Her soul was restored to eternal salvation, and afterward she led a holy life.

Because of this, all of Ita's community and many others who knew of her prophetic power respected her, whether she was absent or present.

The Three Things That Most Please and Displease God

St. Brendan once asked Ita what were the three works most pleasing to God, and the three works most displeasing to him. Ita answered, "Three things that please God most are true faith in God with a pure heart, a simple life with a grateful spirit, and generosity inspired by charity. The three things that most displease God are a mouth that hates people, a heart harboring resentments, and confidence in wealth." St. Brendan and all who were there, hearing that opinion, glorified God in his chosen one.

Ita, the Confessor, Keeps Her Promise

A certain man killed his brother. Touched with remorse, he came to Ita and did penance according to her command. Ita, seeing his devout heart, said: "If you obey my words, you will not have a sudden death, but you will go to eternal life." It happened afterward that he went with his chieftain to fight, for he was a soldier, and the battle went against them, and he was killed. When Ita heard that, she said: "I promised that man that he would have a happy end to his life because he listened to my advice." She said to her attendants: "Go, find him in the devastation, and call upon him in God's name and mine. I believe he will rise and meet you." They did as she said, and the dead man rose from the battle as if he had never been killed. He ran toward those who were searching for him and came with them to Ita. Afterward everything turned out as Ita had promised.

Ita Prepares Her Nuns for Her Death

One day Ita in her venerable old age told her nuns, gathered before her, that her death was near. She spoke to them gently: "MacNisse, the abbot of Clonmacnois, has sent messengers to me that they might bring back water blessed by me for Abbot Aengus, who is very ill. They are hoping he will get well, if he drinks that water. So I will bless that water for them; and, though the messengers are sad, tell them that I have blessed it. For, you see, I will die before they arrive here, and before they return home Aengus will have gone to heaven." And so it happened.

Ita became ill and began to bless and counsel her convent and the clergy and people of Ui Conaill who had received her as their patron. After attaining a great host of virtues, and after many holy people of both sexes had visited her, this most glorious virgin, Ita, happily departed this life in the sight of the holy Trinity and joined the choirs of saints. The angels rejoiced as they came to meet her on the fifteenth of January. Her holy body was buried, after the celebration of Masses, in the monastery she had blessed, in the presence of multitudes from near and far. Numerous miracles were performed, then and later. So Ita, a second Brigit in merits and life, was buried, with our Lord Jesus Christ, living and reigning with God the Father and the Holy Spirit, one God, for ever and ever.

KEVIN
OF GLENDALOUGH

Kevin, or Coemgen, of Glendalough was born sometime in the sixth century. He was one of Ireland's many abbots who was not a bishop, but rather an ordinary priest. He stands in the forefront of the great company of saints of Ireland. He was soul friend with a number of them, including Ciaran of Clonmacnois whom, as we have already seen, he visited on his deathbed. It was Kevin who founded the celebrated monastic city and school at Glendalough, one of the four principal pilgrim sites of Ireland.

Kevin was born in Leinster and was said to have been of royal lineage. As in the case of Maedoc of Ferns, the Venerable Bede, and other saints, Kevin's parents sent him at the age of seven to be educated by monks. Following his ordination, he withdrew to a place of solitude, probably near the Upper Lake by the cave now called "St. Kevin's Bed," until an angel led him to the upper reaches of Glendalough and the Valley of the Two Lakes. He lived as a hermit in that wild region for seven years, clad only in animal skins, sleeping on stones at the water's edge, and nourished on a very frugal diet. According to one version of his Life, such an ascetic lifestyle had its compensations, for "the branches and leaves of the trees sometimes sang sweet songs to him, and heavenly music alleviated the severity of his life." A cattle farmer eventually discovered him in a cave and persuaded him to leave his solitude.

At Disert-Coemgen, where Refert Church now stands, Kevin made a settlement for the disciples who joined him. He eventually moved his community to the glen "where two sparkling rivers meet." Here at Glendalough he made his permanent foundation.

The site, south of Dublin, is still popular with tourists and pilgrims. Located in the shadows of the Wicklow Mountains and surrounded by lakes and forests, it is very beautiful.

St. Kevin died about 618. He was a very popular saint in the Middle Ages. Gerald of Wales once described Kevin as "a great confessor of the faith, and abbot." As the story of the blackbird reveals, Kevin was especially associated with the quality of patience. His feast day is June 3.

Prophecies and the Coming of the "Beautiful Shining Birth"

It was foretold that there would come a high saint, noble and honorable, into Leinster at a place called Glendalough. This saint, the prophecy said, would rescue people from paganism by preaching the word of God; healing lepers, the blind, deaf, and lame, and all kinds of sick folk; raising the dead, putting down the mighty, and lifting up the wretched; driving away plagues; checking thieves, crimes, and strange monsters; and instructing all kinds of perverted folk who opposed the will of God. Patrick, son of Calpurnius, the chief apostle of Erin, prophesied of this Kevin thirty years before his birth that he would build a great monastic city in the glen for the refreshment of companies and strangers, guests and pilgrims, and that he would bring with him to Glendalough some of the earth and relics of the apostles and righteous who are at Rome. It is written that for those who seek to obtain forgiveness of their sins from God, visiting the relics and bed of Kevin with penitence and humility of heart is the same as visiting Rome.

When all these prophecies were fulfilled, the promised one came: Kevin, son of Caemlug and of Caemell, who was the mother of four other children. At the time of Kevin's birth his mother did not experience labor pains, for she bore an innocent, faithful, and righteous offspring. The King of righteousness, the King of heaven, sent twelve angels with golden lamps to Kevin's baptism. And the angels gave him the name Coemgen, that is, "beautiful shining birth."

His Baptism, Fosterage, and Ordination

The angels told the women to take the child to Cronan of Leinster for baptism. Cronan took the child in his arms, baptized him, and gave him the name of Kevin in accordance with the angels' command. Cronan explained to the women that this was an appropriate name for him:

This is the name which God fashioned in heaven,
Which shall cling to the child;
Consider, O women of fair attendance,
that this is his baptismal name, Kevin.

After the baptism, Cronan prophesied that kings and chiefs would believe in Kevin, and that he would do mighty works and miracles. After the baptism the women took Kevin with them to the fort in which he had been born, called the Fort of the White Fountain. He was nurtured there for seven years. God performed great wonders in honor of Kevin, for no matter how great the frost and snow on every side of the fort, it would never penetrate within, and beasts and animals in winter habitually found grass there. Besides this, a brilliantly white cow used to come for the infant's feeding. It was not known whence it came or where it went. In times of fasting and abstinence the child would only suck his mother's breasts once a day.

After seven years at the fort, an angel commanded Kevin to enter an order of monks so that he could get an education and be instructed in manners. He spent a considerable period of time among them, until he was old enough to be a priest. One day when Kevin's tutor was about to say Mass, he told Kevin (who was then a young lad) to go and fetch fire to light the Mass candle. "Give me a vessel in which to bring the embers," said Kevin. When his tutor heard this he became angry and told him to bring the fire in the corner of his mantle. Kevin did so, and when the monk saw the red embers being brought to him in the mantle, without a single thread of the mantle catching fire, he said, "Kevin, it is true that the grace of the Holy Spirit lives in you; I am not worthy that you should wait upon me, but it would be more fitting for me to wait on you." The name of God and of Kevin was magnified through that miracle.

Kevin Chooses the Solitary Life

After Kevin was ordained, an angel told him to go into the desert glen. As he was setting out, the angel came to guide him to the crags located on the western side of the two lakes in Glendalough. There he had no food but the nuts of the forest, the herbs of the earth, and fresh water for drinking. For sleeping he had only a stone for a pillow, a flagstone under him, and a flagstone on each side. He did not even have a cell in which to live. His clothes were the skins of wild animals. He would often go to the crag and to the cave called Kevin's Bed, where he would pray long and fervently to God. He would then return by the forest called Cael Faithe to the north of the lake. He also spent a long time in the lake up to his waist reciting the divine office, sometimes by day, sometimes by night. For seven years he followed this solitary routine, far from the companionship of others. Each day he would cross the lake without any boat to the rock to say Mass and remain there without fear or dread above the lake.

One time, after Kevin had been in his place of solitude for a while, he went into the lake at the end of a snowy night. As he was reciting his psalms, the psalter fell into the lake and sank to some depth. An angel came and said, "Do not grieve." Soon an otter swam up from the bottom of the lake with the book in its mouth and gave it to Kevin. Not a line or letter was blotched or blotted.

The angel told him to return to society to teach and preach the word of God and not to hide himself any longer. But Kevin resisted.

The Farmer Dimma and His Cow

It so happened that a farmer in Leinster named Dimma was destined to help Kevin. Patrick prophesied long before the birth of Kevin that a saint like himself would come to be the patron of Glendalough; God granted that Dimma would discover him, though Kevin continued to conceal himself from people. This is the way it happened.

A herd of Dimma's cows was grazing in the forest in which Kevin was hiding. One of the cows found her way to the hollow in which the saint was being comforted by the angel. The cow kept licking his feet all day. At evening, when she returned home with the rest of the cows, as much milk was milked from her alone as from half the rest of the herd. As often as the herd went into that forest, the same cow would go and lick Kevin's feet, and after coming home in the evening, would again yield a large quantity of milk.

When Dimma and all his company noticed this, they were filled with wonder. Dimma told the herdsman to observe the cow the next day and follow her closely, so that he might discover the location of the excellent pasture. The next day the herdsman followed the cow straight to the tree in whose hollow Kevin was hiding. When he found Kevin, the holy man was weak and feeble, powerless to walk or to move because of his strict asceticism. When he saw the herdsman, Kevin begged him not to reveal to anyone in the world that he was in that hollow.

After the herdsman returned to Dimma, he tried not to tell what he knew about the saint, but Dimma was angry at his herdsman's reluctance to talk and threatened to put him into chains. Finally the herdsman told him how he had discovered Kevin in the hollow of a tree.

When Dimma heard this, great joy possessed him. He and his children made a litter for the saint and set out through the forest to bring him back. Since the road back was rough, Dimma begged Kevin to pray to God to make a way through the woods. Kevin prayed earnestly so that Dimma's children might be able to carry him to where he intended to build a church. The forest gave way on either side, so that an easy passage was made through it. It did so because an angel bent the trees in front of the litter, and, as it passed, returned them to their natural position. Thus they came to the bed of the glen, where the church of Kevin stands today.

Kevin and the Blackbird

Because of the severity of his asceticism, Kevin was accustomed to spend every Lent in a wattled hut with a gray flagstone under him as a bed. His only food was the music of the angels. One Lent a blackbird came from the woods to his hut and hopped on his palm as he lay on the flagstone with his hand stretched out. Kevin kept his hand in that position so the blackbird could build her nest in it. He remained there until she had hatched her brood.

An angel came to visit Kevin, and ordered him to stop the penance in which he was then engaged and to return to society once more. Kevin said, "It is no great thing for me to bear this pain of holding my hand under the blackbird for the sake of heaven's king, for upon the cross of suffering Jesus bore every pain on behalf of Adam's seed." "Come out of the hut," the angel insisted.

"I will not come," Kevin replied, "until I obtain from God the freedom of my successors and my monks, and the maintenance of my churches." The angel placed a little spear of red gold in Kevin's hand and promised him what he requested. As the poet says:

> God gave power to Kevin
> Such as he gave not to every saint in the world:
> On Doomsday to be strong in the assemblies
> Where the children of Adam will be trembling.

Kevin's Pilgrimage to Rome

After settling at Glendalough Kevin went on pilgrimage to Rome. He was well-received by the pope, who gave him permission to establish Glendalough as a place of pilgrimage in perpetuity. He also said that anyone who makes seven pilgrimages to Glendalough would receive the same indulgences and profit as a person who makes one pilgrimage to Rome. As the poet says:

> Great is the pilgrimage of Kevin,
> If people should perform it right;
> To go seven times to that fair city is the same
> As to go once to Rome.

When Kevin returned from Rome he brought back some of the earth of the church of Rome with him and sprinkled it in his own church and in his cemeteries. Because of Kevin's holiness and the rights of pilgrimage guaranteed to Glendalough, a great number of pilgrims began to visit his church from every part of Erin. From then on the four chief places of pilgrimage in Ireland were the Cave of Patrick in Ulster, Croagh Patrick in Connacht, Inis na m-Beo (the Isle of the Living) in Munster, and Glendalough in Leinster, where Kevin's church is.

It is obligatory for everyone who goes on pilgrimage there to abstain from all fighting, quarreling, theft, and rape. Whoever violates the numerous privileges of Kevin's church here below will experience evil in the other world. Kevin left four evil consequences in this world for anyone who ravages his church: tumor, scrofula, anthrax, and madness, without any remedy for them from herb or leech. However, the person who maintains the privileges of Kevin's church will receive three advantages: health, long life, and a happy death.

Kevin's Shame at Not Having Enough to Give

One day as Kevin went to herd his sheep, a great throng of poor people met him who were starved for food. They asked alms of the good man for love of God. Kevin answered them regretfully, saying that he had at that time no food with him there in the wilderness. When the beggars were telling him goodbye, however, Kevin asked them to wait. He then killed seven sheep from his flock and gave them to the beggars, who departed fully satisfied. The next day, when Kevin went to visit his flock, he found that all the sheep were there; not a single one of them was missing to the glory of God. Thus Kevin was freed from the shame that had possessed him when the poor of God asked a favor of him and he had nothing to give them.

The Missing Otter

There was a monastery in Cell Iffin (Eithfin) to which an otter—the one that had fished up Kevin's psalter from the lake—used to bring a salmon each day. One day when Cellach, son of Dimma, saw the otter coming with the salmon in its mouth, he came to the conclusion that the otter's skin would be profitable to the monks and therefore decided to kill the otter. The otter immediately dropped the salmon that was in its mouth, dived into the river, and never showed itself to the monks again. As a consequence, the monks experienced a scarcity of food, so much so that they decided they must go their separate ways. When Kevin saw this, he prayed earnestly to God to reveal why the otter had forsaken the monastery. God heard his prayers and influenced Cellach to go to Kevin and to confess, with regret and penitence, that he was to blame. He admitted that he had had the intention of killing the otter, and that it was at that time that the otter had dived into the river and left the monks. When Kevin heard this he sent Cellach away to do penance for the evil intention that had caused so much harm.

The King's Son and the Fairy Witch; the Doe and the Wolf

It occurred to the king of Ui Faelain to send his young son to Kevin to be baptized and to have him also foster the boy. He sent the child because every son that had been previously born to him had been destroyed by the bright people or fairy courts. When the

---

163

infant came to Kevin to be baptized, a fairy witch named Caineog, along with her attendant women, followed the infant. They were determined to destroy him as they had destroyed every other son of the king of Ui Faelain. When Kevin noticed this, he cursed the women, and they were turned into stones. They still remain in the form of stones on the edge of the lake, which is in the glen.

Now, as to Kevin and the infant, there were neither cows nor calves in the glen at that time, so that finding sustenance and milk to nourish the infant was a great problem and a source of great anxiety for the saint. However, as Kevin looked behind him, he saw a doe with a little fawn following her. When he saw this, he fervently prayed to God to tame the doe, so that she might come and give her milk to the infant. Immediately the doe came to the place, went gently up to Kevin, and dropped her milk into a hollow stone both for the infant and for her own fawn. Every day the doe came to drop her milk into the hollow stone, and every day enough milk was obtained for the infant's nourishment. From then on, that place was called Innis Eilte (the doe's milking stand).

One day, when the doe came to graze in the woods, a wolf came out of a cave, killed the doe's fawn, and devoured it. When Kevin saw this, he ordered the wolf to go gently—in place of the fawn—to the doe, and the wolf did this habitually. So the doe continued to drop her milk on the stone to feed the infant as she formerly did for her fawn, though there was only a wolf standing at her breast. Thus they were frequently together, and in this way the child was nurtured and afterward became a disciple of Kevin. So the name of God was glorified.

Pilgrims Murdered and a Boar Saved

One time when two women were coming on a pilgrimage to Kevin's church, robbers met them at the pass, stripped them, and beheaded them. When Kevin was informed of this, he went quickly to see the women and immediately reattached their heads to their trunks, so that they were restored to life by him. "O Kevin," said the women, "you have healed us, and we give ourselves to you as long as we live." Kevin took the women with him and made devout nuns of them. They remained in the convent, which was near the church of Kevin, and lived the rest of their lives as exemplars in devotion, prayer, and abstinence.

Another time some hunters were hunting a wild boar with their dogs in hot pursuit. As soon as the boar perceived the dogs near him, he set off down the slope of the glen to seek Kevin's protection. Kevin protected the boar and commanded the dogs to stop following him. As he did so, the feet of the dogs stuck to the ground, so that they could not move from that spot in any direction. Shortly after this the hunters came into Kevin's presence. On seeing their dogs fastened to the ground and the boar under Kevin's protection, they were astonished and filled with wonder. Humbly and penitently they asked Kevin to release their dogs and promised him that they would never again pursue this boar. So Kevin let the boar run into the forest, and the name of God was glorified.

Kevin was like this all his life, working miracles until he died at an advanced age of a hundred and twenty-nine years.

MAEDOC OF FERNS

Maedoc, also called Aidan or Mogue, of Ferns was born in Ireland in the last part of the sixth century. A bishop whom hagiographers imaginatively portray as being ordained by the pope himself in Rome, Maedoc is considered the founder of Irish monasteries at Fern in County Wexford, Drumlane in County Cavan, and Rossinver in County Leitrim. He is said to have been educated in Leinster and at St. David's school in Wales. Tradition has it that David and Maedoc were very close soul friends, and that David died in the arms of his friend and former pupil.

It is clear that Maedoc has, like the other Celtic saints, a great capacity for making friends. In the stories that follow we find not only that David is an important mentor to Maedoc, but that Maedoc has close ties with Molaise of Devenish, probably his closest friend, with Columcille, a colleague, with Ita of Killeedy, and even with Brigit of Kildare. The story of his climbing a golden ladder to say farewell to Columcille draws upon a symbol and theme of spiritual progress that recurs often in the history of Judeo-Christian spirituality—from the dream of Jacob (Gn 28:12) to Jesus's own allusion to it (Jn 1:51), on through the writings of Origen, John Climacus, Walter Hilton, Luther, Calvin, and others.

Besides being a soul friend, Maedoc emerges as a powerful saint with strong intuition and a great sensitivity toward those in pain. He is named, as many Native Americans are, after an aspect of nature: "son of the star," a poetic title of honor. A friend of many kinds of animals, Maedoc seems especially to enjoy the company of wolves.

Maedoc died about 626. Although no one knows with certainty where his bones now lie, relics of his are on display in the Armagh Library (a bell) and in the National Museum, Dublin (a shrine). At Ferns today the eucharist is celebrated amid medieval monastic ruins, including the remains of a tower. Maedoc's feast day is January 31.

The Birth of "Son of the Star"

A king succeeded to the province of Connacht whose name was Setna, and his wife was Eithne. They had no offspring, so they entreated God that they might have a son worthy to take their place after them. For this reason they frequently gave alms to the poor and fasted. The saints and righteous friends joined in their prayers, so that they might obtain their request from God. After this the two of them were together, and Eithne saw a vision in which a star fell down from heaven into her mouth. Setna saw the same vision. When they arose, they told each other what they had seen. Then they described the vision to certain wise men who told the couple: "A star guided the kings to Christ to adore him, when he was born in Bethlehem. By the same sign, which has been revealed, a noble son will be born of you who will be filled with the grace and favor of the Holy Spirit." That same night holy Maedoc was conceived in his mother's womb, and it is for this reason that he is called "son of the star."

Not long after, the woman gave birth to a son. On the place where he was born there rested for a long time a bright and dazzling ray from heaven. The holy child was baptized by a devout and chaste priest and by his guardian angel. He was fostered by Ua Dubthaig, who nurtured him zealously and with great affection and kept him from everything unlawful. His foster-mother and nurses, as is the way of loving foster-mothers, gave him a nickname, calling him "my little Aed" (*mo Aed oc*). The name Maedoc stuck to him as a surname to the exclusion of other names.

The Prophecy of Finn Mac Cumaill

The grace of the mighty Lord rested on this child Maedoc beyond all other children of his time. Long before his birth had been foretold by the chief sage and prophet of Ireland, Finn Mac Cumaill. For, just as he was being buried under the ground, Finn put his thumb under his tooth of knowledge so that true knowledge of the future might be revealed to him and ignorance removed. "By my word," said he, "it is good to be buried in a place made holy by the number of harmonious bells, fair learned books, and offerings of the eucharist, which will be celebrated over your head until the world ends." Then he prophesied about Maedoc in a poem:

> Ath Ferna (Ferna's Ford or simply "Ferns")
> The place where excellent Maedoc will be,
> Though many today its litters of wolf cubs,
> Many will be its heavenly cries.
>
> Ath Ferna of the green strand!
> Excellent will be the man who will own it;
> Soul friends will come from there;
> It will be a place dear to God.
>
> Maedoc with his company will come,
> Like the sheen of the sun after showers;
> The son of the star will come,
> A star victorious forever.
>
> It will be an angelic place,
> The place where the fair group will be cooking;
> Maedoc with his company will come,
> Welcome the king whose mighty sepulchre it is.
>
> He will be a strong wealthy prince,
> He will be a flame of fierce doom;
> Maedoc with his company will come,
> He will be a wave over many fords.

Maedoc's Wisdom and Compassion as a Student

When Maedoc's father and mother saw how much favor God had conferred upon their son, they sent him to be educated. The fame of his devotion, the excellence of his studies, his knowledge and his deep wisdom became known to many people.

One day a number of holy men prayed to God to reveal to them the place of their resurrection, for they wished to serve God there. An angel came to them and told them to go where Maedoc was, and he would reveal to them the place of their resurrection.

They went to the saint at the angel's command. Maedoc asked them, "Did you hear the sound of any bell as you came here?" They said that they had not. "Come with me, then, so that I can show you the place of your resurrection." They went with him, and he informed them where their resurrection would be. They remained at that place until their deaths, leading a life of marvelous happiness.

Another day Maedoc was praying deep in the forest when he saw a stag pursued by hounds. The stag stopped by him, and Maedoc threw the corner of his cloak over its horns to protect it from the hounds. When they came running by, they could neither see nor smell the stag, and after they had gone, it ran for safety back into the forest.

The Parting of Friends

Maedoc and Molaise of Devenish were comrades who loved each other very much. One day they sat praying at the foot of two trees. "Ah, Jesus!" they cried, "is it your will that we should part, or that we should remain together until we die?" Then one of the two trees fell to the south, and the other to the north. "By the fall of the trees," they said, "it is clear that we must part." Then they told each other goodbye and kissed each other affectionately. Maedoc went to the south and built a noble monastery at Ferns in the center of Leinster, and Molaise went north to Lough Erne and built a fair monastery at Devenish.

Maedoc Visits Rome and Is Ordained Bishop by the Pope

After the holiness and fame of Maedoc had increased, many people came from every corner of Ireland seeking his guidance and rule. Maedoc desired to leave his own land and country, for he did not want to be honored in this way. He meditated about going on pilgrimage to Rome in order to acquire knowledge and expertise in divine scripture as other saints were doing at that time. He decided to do so, and Caillan the ascetic, Molaise of Devenish, and Ultan of Ardbrecken, among others, accompanied him on this great journey.

When this devout and holy band reached Rome, God performed a wonderful miracle: all of the bells of the place rang out without any human help. The citizens of Rome were filled with great wonder and astonishment and asked about these visitors. The successor of Peter and Paul informed them of the devotion and orthodoxy of this band of worthy saints from Ireland. Three of them, Maedoc the wonderworker, Molaise the modest, and Caillin the devout, were ordained bishops by the pope. It was on this journey that Maedoc received two gifts from the Trinity, which were handed down from heaven and left on the altar of Peter: a crozier and a staff. As a poet said:

> The crozier of Maedoc from the plain of heaven
> The noble patron saint received,
> And he received the staff of Brandub
> From the fair starry vault.

For a whole year they stayed together in Rome acquiring knowledge and receiving honor, respect, and authority from the pope and his clergy and cardinals. Then they promised each other mutual alliance and friendship, said goodbye, and returned to Ireland.

Maedoc Travels to Wales

The Trinity guided Maedoc through the territory of Leinster and from there to Britain, to the place where David of Menevia, the holy bishop, lived. Maedoc was there with David for a long time. During that time the Saxons invaded Britain with a great army. The Britons assembled to oppose them and sent messengers to David to ask him to send Maedoc to them to bless their army and consecrate their battalion.

Maedoc went at David's bidding to where the Britons and Saxons were confronting one another. In numbers, the Britons were no match for the Saxons, but Maedoc prayed on behalf of the Britons, and the Saxons fled with the Britons pursuing them. For seven days the Britons slaughtered and butchered the Saxons, and not one man of the Britons fell by the hands of the Saxons all that time. Because of God's favor and Maedoc's miracles, no Saxons invaded Britain while Maedoc was there.

After many miracles were performed in Britain, Maedoc asked permission of David to return to Ireland. He then began his return journey to Ireland together with his disciples. As he drew near to the Irish coast, he saw robbers on one side of a road, robbing and killing pilgrims. Maedoc told his companions, "Let us hurry to the pilgrims." Then he rang his bell and the robber chief heard it. "That is the sound of a devout and holy man's bell," the robber said, "and he rings his bell to tell us to stop our work." After that they let the pilgrims be.

Later, when Maedoc was walking by the ocean with his comrades, he said to them, "I am sorry that I did not ask my master, David, who should be my soul friend in Ireland." His disciples began to prepare a ship, but the boatmen were not willing to return to Wales. Maedoc leaped out of the boat and walked from wave to wave until an angel met him. "You need no soul friend but the God of the Elements," the angel said, "for he understands the thoughts and secrets of every person." So Maedoc returned again to Ireland and built a noble church where he landed.

Maedoc's Compassion for Wolves

Maedoc built a church in the place called Disert nDairbre (Oakwood Hermitage), and was there sometime with his disciples. The brothers had two cows and a calf there. One day Maedoc was alone in his cell when he saw some wolves approaching. They circled him gently, and he understood that they were asking for food. He was moved to compassion for them and gave the calf to them to eat it. But one of the brothers said to him, "The cows will not give milk without the calf." Maedoc said to him, "Bend your head toward me so that I may bless it. When the cows see it, they will give their milk obediently to you." As so it was that whenever the cows saw the head of the brother, they would suddenly lick it and then give their milk to him.

On another occasion Maedoc came to the monastery named Shanbo, at the foot of the hill called Mount Leinster. As he was going along the road, a mother wolf, wretched, weak, and starving, happened to meet him. It came up to him gently as if seeking his attention. Maedoc asked a lad who had joined him on the road whether he had anything he could give the wolf. The boy said that he had one loaf and a piece of fish. Maedoc took this from him and threw it to the wolf. The boy was disturbed at seeing this and said that he was afraid of what his master would do to him. Maedoc said, "Bring me some of the leaves of the forest." The boy did as he had been told. Then Maedoc blessed the foliage, and it was turned into a loaf and a fish, which he gave to the lad.

Maedoc Receives the Gift of Ferns

Once the king of Ui Cennselaig was on a raiding expedition. He met Maedoc and gave him alms and proceeded to his monastery. Disease and a grievous illness, however, overtook the king, so that it seemed to him as if his spirit departed from him. He seemed to see hell and horrible animals attacked him. As one of these dragged the king with its breath into its very mouth, he saw the poor man, Maedoc, putting the alms he had given to him into the beast's mouth. Even that, however, did not stop the beast from hanging on tightly—until the saint brought his staff down hard on the beast's mouth.

The king awoke from this nightmare and told everyone what he had seen. "Send for Maedoc," they said, "and you will learn everything from him." "No, it is better that I should go to the servant of God," the king said, and he went to where Maedoc was. "This is the man to whom I gave the alms," the king said, "and who freed me from the mouth of the beast." And the king gave him Ferns in perpetuity, and he built a church there.

The inhabitants complained to Maedoc that the place was waterless. "Dig at that tree yonder," said Maedoc, "and you will find a spring." They did as he had said, and a thin bright stream of green blue-edged water began to flow along the boundary of the land.

Maedoc Visits Old Friends and Climbs the Golden Ladder

Sometime later Maedoc was in the district of Munster near Ita's monastery. He had decided to go and visit his father-confessor Molua mac Oiche when he heard the bells of Ita's place ringing. Maedoc asked why the bells were ringing, and a voice in the air replied that a foster-child of Ita, a virgin who was dearly loved and a favorite of hers, had just died.

Ita heard that Maedoc was in the neighborhood and sent a messenger to him inviting him to come and restore the woman to life. Maedoc told one of the disciples to go to the place, take Maedoc's staff, and lay it on the woman's chest. This was done, and she arose at once in the presence of all. Everyone who saw or heard of this miracle gave glory to God and to Maedoc. Later Maedoc went west to Clonmacnois to bind his alliance and covenant with Ciaran and his monks.

Sometime later Maedoc was teaching a student by a high cross at the monastery of Ferns. The student saw him mount a golden ladder reaching from earth to heaven. Maedoc climbed the ladder, and when he returned sometime later, the student could not look in his face because of the brilliance of his countenance. Maedoc told him, "Never tell anyone about what you have seen." "If that is what you want," the student replied, "I will not tell anyone." "Columcille has died," Maedoc told him, "and I went to meet him with the family of heaven. He was my own soul friend in this world, so I wanted to pay him my respects." The student told this story only after Maedoc's death, when he had become an adult and a holy man himself.

Maedoc's Death and His Appearance with Brigit

When Maedoc was at Ferns, an angel of the Lord revealed to him that the end of his life was approaching. He told him to leave his churches and his chosen sanctuaries and to go to the place of his resurrection and to the site of his burial. Maedoc did as he was told, leaving Ferns in the hands of his successors. He went to Drumlane and did the same, blessing the place and bidding farewell. When he arrived at Rossinver, over 150 saints and holy virgins came to the scene of his death and departure. He received communion, and then, after healing folk of every affliction and disease who came to him in the name of the Trinity, he sent his spirit to heaven. Hosts of angels came to meet him and with melodious songs to carry his soul to Paradise.

There was also a man in Leinster who had lain sick for thirty years. He saw a vision of a chariot coming to him from heaven with the aged cleric, accompanied by a virgin, standing in it. "Who are you?" asked the man. "I am Maedoc," said the cleric, "and this is Brigit. Tomorrow is my day, and the day after tomorrow is Brigit's day, and we come from on high to glorify Jesus on our feast days. Be ready," the saint warned, "for you will die on the third day, and your soul will obtain the heavenly kingdom." The holy man, whose name was Fintan, went to Kildare, a church of Brigit's, and related to the people the vision he had seen. He died the third day as Maedoc had predicted, and he passed to heaven.

MONESAN OF BRITAIN

Nothing is known of this courageous woman except the story of her that appears in the seventh-century *Life of Saint Patrick* written by Muirchu, a hagiographer at Armagh. The daughter of a British king, she persisted in her search for God until her parents finally brought her to Ireland, where she was baptized by Patrick. Monesan is one of countless women who have contributed much to the spread and vitality of Christianity and yet have received little recognition.

Monesan's Passionate Search for God

At that time, when all of Britain was still frozen in the chill of unbelief, a certain king's remarkable daughter, called Monesan, was filled with the Holy Spirit. When someone asked for her hand in marriage, she did not consent. Not even when floods of water were poured over her could she be forced to do what she did not want. In the midst of beatings and drenchings with water she used to ask her mother and her nurse whether they knew the maker of the wheel by which all the world is illuminated. When she received an answer that the sun's maker was he whose throne was in heaven, and when she was repeatedly pressured to marry someone, she would reply, enlightened by the shining advice of the Holy Spirit, "I will never do that." For through nature she searched for the maker of all creation, following in this the example of the patriarch Abraham.

Deliberating in their great sorrow, her parents decided to follow a plan given to them by God. They had heard that a man named Patrick was visited by the eternal God every seventh day. So they travelled over to Ireland with their daughter and after great effort met Patrick. He asked his visitors why they had come. The travellers began to cry out and say: "It is because of our daughter's passionate desire to see God that we have been forced to come to you." Then Patrick, filled with the Holy Spirit, raised his voice and said to her: "Do you believe in God?" Monesan replied: "I do." Then he washed her in the holy baptism of water and the Holy Spirit. Immediately afterward she fell to the ground and gave up her spirit into the hands of the angels. She was buried on the spot where she died. Then Patrick prophesied that after twenty years her body would be removed with all honor from there to a neighboring oratory. This is in fact what happened later, and the relics of this woman from across the sea were venerated there for many years.

Non, or Nonna, the mother of St. David of Wales, was one of many Celtic missionaries who travelled from Ireland and Wales through Cornwall and on to continental Europe. Little is known about her except what appears in a late eleventh-century *Life of St. David* by Rhigyfarch, the eldest son of a bishop of St. David's. In that hagiography we find that, despite the pious words used to describe David's birth and early childhood, his mother, who may have been a nun, was raped, and he was evidently raised fatherless. Both mother and son, however, went on to become the two best-known and loved saints of Wales.

Non left her native land about 527 for Cornwall, where at Alternon there is a beautiful church and holy well named after her. A fine Celtic cross, similar to numerous others in Cornwall, stands by the church gate. It probably dates back to the time of St. Non herself. According to legends, she eventually died in Brittany, where her tomb survives at Finistere. Her trust in God and her courageous dedication to serving the church as a missionary are two of her most admirable attributes.

Non's feast day is celebrated in Wales on March 3, two days after her son's. At Alternon, in Cornwall, it is celebrated on June 25.

The Rape of Non and David's Birth

While Sanctus, king of the people of Ceredigion, was passing through the Dyfed countryside, he met a maiden called Nonita (little nun) who was exceedingly beautiful, a modest virgin. Inflamed with desire, the king raped her. She, neither before nor after this occasion had intercourse with any man, but continued in chastity of mind and body, leading a most faithful life. From this time on, after conceiving, she lived only on bread and water. A small meadow lay in that place where she was violated and where she conceived. By divine favor this meadow was covered with heavenly dew. At the time of conception, two large stones also appeared in that meadow, one at her head and one at her feet. Thus, the earth herself, rejoicing in the conceiving, opened its bosom, both in order to preserve the young woman's modesty, and also to declare beforehand the significance of her offspring.

Non, as her womb was growing, followed the usual custom and entered a church in order to offer alms and oblations for the child's birth. Here she met a certain teacher who was preaching the word to the people. As Non entered, he suddenly became dumb as if silenced by an obstruction in the throat. When asked by the congregation why he had broken off his sermon and become silent, he replied: "I can talk to you in ordinary conversation, but I am unable to preach. Go outside and allow me to remain here alone to see if I can preach under those conditions." The congregation went outside, but Non concealed herself and hid in a corner. She stayed behind not intending to disobey the injunction, but because of an intense thirst for the word of life. She also wished to assert the privilege of one so great as her offspring.

A second time the preacher, although striving with wholehearted effort, could do nothing, as if he were prevented by heaven. Terrified by this, he now cried with a loud voice, "I adjure anyone who may be hiding from me, to reveal himself from his place of concealment and to make himself known." Then Non said in reply, "I am hiding here." Inspired by divine providence he said, "Go out, and let the congregation re-enter the church!" They did so, and he preached in his usual manner with unfettered tongue.

Non, when asked, confessed that she was pregnant. It was clearly evident to all that the child she was about to bring into the world was one who, in virtue of the privilege of his dignity, the splendor of his wisdom, and the eloquence of his preaching, would excel all the teachers of Britain. This was corroborated by the excellences of David's subsequent life.

Meanwhile, there was a certain ruler living nearby. He learned from the prophecies of his druids that a boy would be born within his realm whose power would extend over the whole country. This man, intent only on earthly things and finding his highest good in these lowest pursuits, was tormented by a mighty hatred and jealousy. Discovering from the pronouncements of the druids where the boy was to be born, he said, "Let me keep watch by myself upon that site for as many days as necessary, and whomever I find resting there, even for a short time, will die, slain by my own sword." As had been foreordained, the nine months came around, and the time for the birth drew near.

One day Non went out along that very road, leading to the place of the birth. The tyrant was keeping watch in accordance with the druid's prophecy. Driven by the approaching time of the birth, the mother sought the predicted place. Suddenly a great storm arose, with such vivid flashes of lightning, such terrifying peals of thunder, and so excessive a downpour of hail and rain, that no one could go out of doors. The place where Non lay groaning in labor, however, shone with so brilliant a light that it glistened in God's presence as if lit by the sun, though it was obscured by clouds. In her labor Non had a certain stone near her on which she leaned with her hands when overtaken by her pains. The marks of her hands, as though impressed on wax, have been identified in that stone for those who have gazed upon it. It even broke in half in sympathy with the mother's agony. On that spot where David was born a church has been built, in the foundations of which this stone lies concealed.

PATRICK
OF ARMAGH

St. Patrick, the patron saint of Ireland, is the most famous of the Celtic saints. He was born about 390 near the west coast of England or Wales. Like many of the earliest saints, we do not have a great deal of factual information about him. Two autobiographical writings, however, have survived: *Confessio*, which he wrote toward the end of his life to defend himself against detractors at home who were questioning his integrity, and a *Letter to Coroticus*, in which he protested the captivity and martyrdom of some of his Irish converts by a Welsh chieftain. Both writings, along with the stories written by hagiographers about him, give us insight into his passionate personality and his great love of the Irish, whom he adopted as his own sons and daughters.

Patrick's father was a deacon and his grandfather a priest. While still a youth he was captured by pirates and taken to Ireland, where he lived for six years as a slave. It was there, while tending sheep in solitude, that he had a religious conversion. Helped by inner voices and dreams, Patrick escaped and eventually returned to his own country. Some years later he had another vivid dream in which a figure named Victor brought letters from the Irish, telling him to "come back and walk with us once more." Patrick interpreted this dream as a genuine call from God revealing his missionary vocation. Later generations identified his dream figure, Victor, with a guardian angel and soul friend who guided Patrick throughout his life.

In 432 Patrick landed on Ireland's shores and as a missionary-bishop spent the rest of his life making converts and organizing the church, primarily in the north. He died near Armagh in 461. Although a huge boulder bears his name in the cemetery at

Downpatrick today, no one knows where his body is buried. At Armagh two churches face each other from two different hills: one, the Church of Ireland, stands at the original windswept site associated with Patrick's monastery; the other, the Roman Catholic Cathedral, houses one of the richest collections of Celtic religious art. Patrick's feast day, as almost everyone knows, is celebrated March 17.

Patrick's Early Life and Captivity in Ireland

Patrick, who was also called Sochet, was born in Britain, the son of the deacon Calpurnius, whose father, as Patrick himself says, was the priest Potitus, who came from the town of Bannavem Taburniae, not far from our sea. We have discovered for certain and beyond any doubt that this township is Ventre, and the mother who bore him was named Concessa.

At the age of sixteen the boy, with others, was captured and brought to this island of barbarians and was kept as a slave in the household of a certain cruel pagan king. He spent six years in captivity, in accordance with the Jewish custom, in fear and trembling before God, as the psalmist says, and in many vigils and prayers. He used to pray a hundred times a day and a hundred times a night, giving gladly to God what is due God and to Caesar what is due to Caesar. Patrick began to fear God and to love the Lord Almighty, for up to that time he had no knowledge of the true God, but at this point the Spirit became alive within him.

After many hardships there, after enduring hunger and thirst, cold and nakedness, after pasturing flocks, after visits from Victor, an angel sent to him by God, after great miracles known to almost everyone, after divine prophecies in the twenty-third year of his life, Patrick left the earthly, pagan king and his works and received the heavenly, eternal God. He then sailed for Britain by God's command and was accompanied by the Holy Spirit. With him were barbarian strangers and pagans who worshipped many false gods.

He Finds a Mentor in Gaul

When Patrick was thirty years old he set out to visit and pay his respects to the apostolic see, that is, to the head of all the churches in the whole world. He wanted to learn and understand

182

the divine wisdom and holy mysteries to which God called him and to fulfill them so that he might preach and confer divine grace on foreign peoples by converting them to faith in Christ.

So he crossed the southern British sea and began his journey through Gaul with the intention of eventually crossing the Alps, as he had resolved in his heart. He came to the home of a very holy bishop, Germanus, who ruled in the city of Auxerre, the greatest lord in almost all of Gaul. Patrick stayed with him for quite some time, just as Paul sat at the feet of Gamaliel. In all humility, patience, and obedience he learned, loved, and treasured wholeheartedly knowledge, wisdom, purity, and every benefit to soul and spirit, with great fear and love for God, in goodness and singleness of heart and chaste in body and spirit.

When Patrick had spent a considerable time there—some say forty years, others thirty—that most faithful friend Victor, who had foretold everything to him in a large number of dreams, told Patrick that the time was at hand for him to come and fish with the net of the gospel for the wild, barbarian peoples whom God had sent him to teach. "The sons and daughters of the forest of Foclut are calling you."

And so, when a suitable opportunity came about, with God's help to accompany him, Patrick set out on the journey he had already begun, to do the work for which he had long been prepared—the work of the gospel.

Patrick's Confrontation with the Druids at the Court of Tara

So Patrick returned to Ireland and travelled to Tara, the home of the Irish kings. As he prepared to celebrate holy Easter, he kindled the divine fire with its bright light and blessed it. As it gleamed in the darkness it was seen by almost all the inhabitants of the flat plain. It was also seen from Tara, and everyone wondered at the sight. King Loiguire called together the elders, councilors, and druids and said to them: "What is this? Who is it who has dared to commit this sacrilege in my kingdom? Let him be put to death." They all replied that they did not know who had done it, but the druids answered: "O king, may you live forever! This fire, which we see and which was lit this night before one was lit in your palace of Tara, will never be put out unless it is put out

183

this very night; what is more, it will surpass all the fires of our customs, and he who has kindled it and the kingdom brought upon us by him who has kindled it on this night will overpower us all and you. It will seduce all the people of your kingdom, and all kingdoms will yield to it. It will spread over the whole country and will reign for ever and ever."

King Loiguire was deeply disturbed at these words, as was Herod of old, and all the city of Tara with him. In reply he said: "It will not be so; no, we shall now go to see what is going on and to put an end to this matter. We shall arrest and put to death those who are committing such sacrilege against our kingdom." So yoking twenty-seven chariots, as the tradition of the gods demanded, and taking these two druids, Lucetmael and Lochru, the best of all for this confrontation, Loiguire left Tara at dawn and proceeded to the burial place of the men of Fiacc. When Patrick rose and saw their chariots and horses approaching, he went to them, rather appropriately singing with heart and voice this verse of the Psalmist: "Some may go in chariots and some on horses, but we shall walk in the name of our God." They did not rise as he approached. One, however, with God's help, refused to obey the druid's words. His name was Ercc, son of Daeg, whose relics are now venerated in the city called Slane. He rose to meet Patrick. Patrick blessed him, and Ercc believed in the eternal God.

They then began to talk with one another, and one of the two druids, called Lochru, was insolent to the saint's face and had the effrontery to disparage the Catholic faith in the most arrogant terms. Patrick glared fiercely at him as he spoke, as once Peter did with Simon, and then, with strange power, he shouted aloud and confidently addressed the Lord: "O Lord, who can do all things and in whose power all things lie, who sent me here, may this impious man who blasphemes your name be now carried up out of here and die without delay." At these words the druid was carried up into the air and then dropped outside from above. He fell headfirst, crashing his skull against a stone, and was smashed to pieces. As he died before their eyes, the pagans were afraid.

The king with his followers was angry with Patrick at this and determined to kill him. He ordered his men: "Lay hands on this fellow who is about to destroy us." When holy Patrick saw that the ungodly pagans were about to rush him, he rose and said in a clear voice: "May God arise and his enemies be scattered and those who hate him flee from his face." Immediately darkness fell on them, and there was a horrible sort of upheaval with the ungodly attacking one another. As they struggled a great earthquake locked their chariot-axles together and drove them off violently. The chariots and horses rushed away at breakneck speed over the flat plain, until in the end only a few of them escaped to the mountain Monduirn. In this disaster seven times seven men perished through the curse of Patrick, and there remained only the king himself and three other survivors, that is, his queen and two of the Irish. All of them were very frightened.

The king came, compelled by fear, and bowed his knee before the saint and pretended to worship the God he did not want to worship. After they had parted, the king, going a little way off, called holy Patrick over on some pretext, with the intention of killing him some way or other. But Patrick, aware of the wicked king's thoughts, first blessed his companions (eight men and a boy) in the name of Jesus Christ, and then came to the king. The king counted them as they approached, and suddenly they disappeared from the king's sight. The pagans saw only eight deer with a fawn heading for the wilds. And King Loiguire, saddened, frightened, and humiliated, returned at dawn to Tara with the few survivors.

The following day, that is, Easter Day, the kings and princes and druids were at table with Loiguire. This was their most important feast day, and they ate and drank wine in the palace of Tara. Some were talking, while others were thinking about what had happened. Patrick, accompanied by only five companions, entered through the closed doors, as we read that Christ did, in order to vindicate and to preach the holy faith at Tara before all the nations. As he entered the banquet hall at Tara, only one of the number rose at his approach, Dubthach maccu Lugir, an excellent poet.

While they were all feasting, the druid Lucetmail, who had been involved in the clash during the night, was provoked to fight Patrick because of his colleague's death. To start the contest off, as the others looked on, he poured something from his own goblet into Patrick's cup to test his reaction. Holy Patrick, seeing this kind of test, blessed his cup in the sight of all, and the liquid froze like ice. When the cup was turned upside down, only the drop the druid had poured in fell out. Patrick blessed the cup a second time, and the liquid returned to its natural state. Everyone present was amazed. After a little while the druid said: "Let us work miracles on this vast plain." And Patrick asked: "What sort of miracles?" The druid replied: "Let us bring snow over the land." And Patrick said: "I refuse to bring what is contrary to God's will." And the druid said: "I shall bring it in the sight of all." Then he began his magical spells and brought snow upon the whole plain, deep enough to reach people's waists. All who saw this were astonished. Then Patrick said: "All right, we can see this; now remove it." The druid replied: "I cannot take it away before this time tomorrow." The saint said: "You can do evil, but not good. It is not like that with me." Then he blessed the entire plain, and in no time the snow disappeared, without rain, mist, or wind. And the crowds cheered and were greatly amazed and touched in their hearts.

Soon after, the druid invoked demons and brought very thick darkness on the land as a sign. The people all muttered angrily. Patrick said: "Drive away the darkness." But the druid could not. The saint then gave a blessing in prayer, and suddenly the darkness was driven away and the sun shone. All the onlookers shouted aloud and gave thanks. After this contest between the druid and Patrick in the king's presence, the king said to them: "Throw your books into water, and we shall venerate the one whose books come out unscathed." Patrick answered, "I shall do so." But the druid said, "I refuse to undergo a trial by water with this man, for he considers water to be his God." (He had heard, no doubt, that Patrick baptized with water.) So the king replied, "Then agree to ordeal by fire." Patrick responded: "I am ready." Again the druid refused, saying: "This man worships in alternate years now water, now fire as his God." And the saint said: "That is not true. But you go yourself, with one of my students, into a divided and closed house. You shall wear my garment, and my student will wear yours. Together you will both be set on fire and be judged in the presence of the high God."

This plan was accepted, and a house was built for them, with one half made of green wood and the other of dry wood. The druid was sent into the green part of the house, with Patrick's robe round him, and one of Patrick's students, a boy called Benignus, went into the dry part of the house wearing the druid's cloak. The house was closed up from the outside and was set on fire before the whole crowd. And in that hour it so happened that, as Patrick prayed, the fire's flames consumed the druid in the green half of the house, leaving only Patrick's robe untouched by the fire.

Benignus, on the other hand, was more fortunate, as was the dry half of the house. The fire did not touch him and brought him neither pain nor discomfort. Only the cloak of the druid was burnt in accordance with God's will.

And holy Patrick said to the king: "Unless you believe now, you will die at once, for God's wrath will come down upon your head." And the king was terrified, his heart trembling, as was his entire city. So King Loiguire assembled the elders and all his council and said to them, "It is better for me to believe than to die." And on his followers' advice, he believed that day and turned to the eternal Lord God, as did many others on that occasion.

Holy Patrick, following the Lord Jesus' command, left Tara, and went forth to teach all peoples, baptizing them in the name of the Father and the Son and the Holy Spirit. He preached everywhere, the Lord working with him and confirming his word by the miracles that followed.

Patrick's Soul Friend, Victor

An angel used to come to Patrick regularly on the seventh day of every week. As one person talks to another, so Patrick enjoyed the angel's conversation. Even when he had fallen into captivity and spent six years in servitude, the angel came thirty times to meet him, and he enjoyed the angel's counsels and their conversations before he left Ireland as a young man. He used to pray a hundred times during the day, and a hundred times during the night. One day, when tending swine, he lost them; the angel came to him and showed him where the swine were. One day after the same angel had talked to him about many things he placed his foot on the rock of Scirit, opposite Sliab Miss, and ascended in Patrick's presence. The footprint of the angel remained in the rock. That place, where the angel had spoken with him thirty times, became a place of prayer where the faithful very joyfully obtained the things for which they prayed.

Coroticus Is Punished for His Crimes

News had been brought to Patrick of a wicked act by a certain British king named Coroticus, a cruel and evil ruler. This man had no equal as a persecutor and murderer of Christians. Patrick tried to call him back to the way of truth by a letter, but he scorned

Patrick's salutary exhortations. When this was reported to Patrick, he prayed to the Lord and said, "My God, if it is possible, expel this godless man from this world and from the next." Not much time had elapsed after this when Coroticus heard somebody recite a poem saying that he should abandon his royal throne, and all the men who were dearest to him chimed in. Suddenly before their eyes, in the middle of a public place, the king was ignominiously changed into a fox, went off, and since that day and hour, like water that flows away, was never seen again.

The Gift of Armagh

There was in the country of Airthir a rich and respected man called Daire. Patrick asked him to give him some place for his religious observances. The rich man said to the saint, "What place do you want?" "I want you to give me that piece of high ground called Willow Ridge, and I shall build a place there," answered Patrick. The man refused to give the saint that high ground but gave him another site on lower ground now called the Martyrs' Graveyard near Armagh. Patrick lived there with his followers.

After some time a groom of Daire brought his remarkable horse to graze in the Christians' grassy meadow. Patrick was annoyed that the horse was brought onto his ground and said, "Daire has acted stupidly in sending his brute beasts to disturb the little ground that he gave to God." But the groom like a deaf man did not hear, and like a dumb man not opening his mouth he said nothing. He let the horse loose there for the night and went away. When the groom came back the following morning to see his horse, he found it dead. Returning home he sadly reported to his master, "Look, that Christian has killed your horse, since the disturbance annoyed him." Daire replied, "Let him be killed too—go now and slay him."

But as they went outside death fell on Daire quick as a flash. His wife said: "This death is because of the Christian. Someone go quickly and have his blessings brought back to us, and you will be saved; and let those who have gone off to kill him be stopped and recalled." Two men went off to the Christian, and concealing what had actually happened said to him, "Look, Daire has been taken ill; let something be brought to him from you so that he may be cured." St. Patrick, knowing what had happened, said, "To be sure." He blessed some water and gave them it, saying, "Go, sprinkle your horse with this water and take it with you." They did so, and the horse came back to life. Then they sprinkled Daire with the water and he was cured immediately.

Afterward Daire came to honor Patrick, bringing with him a wonderful bronze bowl from across the sea. "Here is your bowl," he said to Patrick. "For you are a firm, steadfast man. What is more, I give you, as far as it is mine to give, that piece of ground you once requested; live there." That city is now called Armagh.

Patrick's Place of Resurrection

Now after these great marvels the day of Patrick's death and of his going to heaven drew near. With his companions, he began to go to Armagh in order that his resurrection might be there. Beside the road, however, a bush was ablaze, but it did not burn down, as had happened to Moses before. In the bush was the angel Victor, who often used to visit Patrick. This Victor sent another angel to Patrick to stop him from going where he wanted to go. He said to him: "Why do you go on a journey without Victor's guidance? Victor calls you. Change your route and go to him." So Patrick changed his route as he had been told and asked what he should do. The angel answered, "Return to the place from which you came. It is there you shall die, and not in Armagh. But it has been granted you by God that your dignity and your preeminence, your piety and your teaching shall be in Armagh as if you yourself were alive there." Patrick said:

It is Armagh that I love,
A deep thorpe, a dear hill,
A fortress which my soul haunts.

When the hour of his death approached, Patrick received the sacrament from the hands of bishop Tassach for his journey to a blessed life.

During the first night of his funeral rites angels kept the vigil of his body with prayers and the singing of psalms. All those who had come for the vigil slept on that night. During the other nights, however, men watched by the body, saying prayers and singing psalms. After the angels had returned to heaven they left behind them a sweet scent as of honey and a fragrance of sweetness as of wine, so as to fulfill what has been said in the benedictions of the patriarch Jacob, "Behold, the scent of my son is like the scent of a fruitful field which the Lord has blessed."

The angel had told Patrick, "So that your relics will not be removed from the ground, one cubit of earth will be placed on your body." That this was done at the command of God was shown when a church was being built above the body. The men who dug up the ground saw fire burst forth from his tomb and retreated in fear of the fiery flames.

SAMThANN
OF CLONBRONEY

Samthann, or Safan, was an important abbess of the monastery at Clonbroney in Ireland. Some credit her with the founding of that monastery, although one tradition gives the credit to St. Patrick, while another says that St. Brigit's followers accomplished it. A story found in a collection of writings from the Monastery of Tallaght, outside of Dublin, shows that she was a soul friend of Maelruain, one of the key leaders of the Celi De, a reform movement of the eighth and ninth centuries that sought to revitalize Celtic spirituality. We know little about Samthann's early life, except that she was born in Ulster, that her distinguished foster-father was a king of Ireland, and that she was married before becoming a nun. When Samthann entered the monastic community, her responsibilities included conducting the financial affairs of the monastery. This office evidently gave her the ability to be generous to the lepers and guests, pilgrims and penitents who visited there, as well as members of her own community.

Samthann's many abilities are referred to in the stories that follow. She appears in dreams to offer direction and advice; she has an ability to heal those who come to her for help; she goes into an ecstatic state while praying for the soul of her friend Flann. Above all, Samthann is portrayed as a woman of prayer, someone who knocked frequently "at the doors of divine mercy."

Samthann died in 739. Nothing remains of her monastery today, and there does not seem to be any local cult to honor her name. For those who appreciate the soul friend tradition, however, Samthann continues to teach and guide by her example. Her feast day is December 19.

Samthann's Ancestry, Marriage, and Decision to Become a Nun

Samthann's father's name was Diamramus, and her mother's, Columba. As she matured her foster-father, Cridan, king of the Ui Coirpri, gave her in marriage to a nobleman. Before the marriage solemnities were celebrated, the nobleman saw at midnight something like a ray of the sun extended through the roof of the house onto the bed in which Samthann was sleeping with the king's two daughters. Amazed by the unusual vision of light at such an hour, he rose immediately and, advancing toward his spouse's bed, found that her face was illumined by that ray. He was very happy that he was gifted with a spouse who was surrounded by heavenly light.

The following night, when the solemnities had been celebrated, both were entering the marriage bed, as is customary, when her husband said to her, "Undress yourself so that we may become one." But she replied, "I ask you to wait until all who are in this house are asleep." The husband agreed. After a short time tiredness overcame him. Then Samthann gave herself to prayer, knocking at the doors of divine mercy so that God might keep her virginity unblemished. And God heard her prayer, for about midnight that town in which they lived seemed to outsiders to be on fire. A flame of extraordinary magnitude was seen ascending from the mouth of the holy virgin to the roof of the house. A mighty cry was raised outside in the town and those who were asleep within were awakened. Together, they hastened to extinguish the fire.

In the meantime the holy virgin Samthann hid herself in a cluster of ferns nearby. The fire vanished immediately without doing any damage to the town. When morning came, her foster-father, the king, set out to look for her. When he found her, she said to the king, "Was your town burned last night?" The king replied, "No." She said, "I thank God that it was not burned." Then she spoke to the king again, "Why did you wish to give this poor servant of the Almighty God to any spouse without her consent?" The king replied, "All right, I will not give you to a man, but let you be the judge." Samthann said, "This is my decision: as of now you give me as a spouse to God and not to man." Then the king said, "We offer you to God, the spouse whom you choose." Then she, with her husband's permission, entered the monastery of the virgin Cognat, where she remained for a time.

Samthann's Generosity

One day the holy virgin Samthann rose very early and heard the voice of a certain leper at the other side of the pond. He was asking in a loud voice to be brought across the water. Responding to his wishes, the holy virgin guided a boat with her staff and brought him across. Since he was complaining of his poverty and lack of clothing, she gave him a cow with a calf and her cloak, as though she were another St. Martin of Tours. When she asked him from where he had come, he said that he had come from holy Ultan's monastery. The cow and calf and cloak that leper received were later found in the cattle shed.

On another occasion when she was the dispenser of the goods of the monastery of Earnaidhe, it happened that due to her blessing a container of butter sufficed for the use of both nuns and guests. A certain member of the community, newly converted from the world, however, entered the cellar of the sisters. Samthann did not know this. The novice saw the container of butter, which was almost full, and said to herself, "This butter, it seems, will never be totally diminished." When she had gone out, taking the butter with her, the holy virgin Samthann entered that place and found the container empty. She was very surprised upon seeing it and wondered what could have happened. Filled with prophetic insight, she said, "This place will never be wealthy." And what she said of the place was truly fulfilled.

She Becomes Abbess of the Monastery at Clonbroney

At that time the holy virgin Funecha, reputed to be the foundress of the monastery of Clonbroney, saw holy Samthann in a dream in the form of a spark of fire which, as it approached, sprang up into a great flame, burning the entire monastery. Relating the dream to her sisters, she explained it by saying, "Samthann, burning with the fire of the Holy Spirit, will make this place shine with the splendor of her miracles and the power of her merits." So Funecha sent for Samthann and made her abbess of her monastery.

When Samthann had become abbess, she wished first to build an oratory of smooth wood. So she sent carpenters and other workmen to cut down trees in the forest nearby. While most of the other workers had an abundance of food, one of the carpenters had very little. He thought to himself: "Oh, if only we had forty wheat loaves with butter, cheese, and milk! That supply would be enough for all of us." The man was not denied any part of his wish, for by the merits of Samthann, he saw all that he had wished for appear before him. Then the servant of Christ said with a little smile, "Was not your heart's desire fulfilled?" And he responded, "Yes, there is neither too much nor too little." Then everyone was fed adequately, and all gave thanks to God and to his servant.

The Power of Samthann's Prayers

On another occasion holy Samthann sent messengers to a certain king named Kennedy, who held a captive in chains. She requested that he might free the man, but the proud king, despising her prayers, did not accede to them. Again she sent messengers, whom she had instructed, "If he will not allow the prisoner to be freed from his chains, say to the captive, 'In the name of the Holy Trinity, you will be loosed from your chains and come safely to Samthann, the servant of the same Trinity.'" Since the king remained obstinate in his impiety, they spoke to the prisoner as the servant of Christ had commanded. His reply to them was, "I believe that as she has said, so it will be." When the king heard this, he doubled the chains on the prisoner, and the following night he placed eight guards at the gate of the prison and the same number at the gate of the town. At midnight the prisoner, freed by divine help, arose. When he was passing the first guards, they said to him, "Who are you, going about like this?" He replied, "I am Fallamain, who was in chains" (that was the prisoner's name). The guards said to him, "If you were that man, you would not be appearing in public like that." Then the former prisoner, in order to avoid the second watch, climbed over a wall and escaped. On the third day, without the slightest harm, he reached holy Samthann.

By the power of her prayer, the same virgin tamed beasts of a nearby pond. They had previously caused havoc with people and the flocks, but after that they did no more harm.

The same virgin—with the help of only one cow—once fed fifty guests until they were completely satisfied. At the time she had nothing else with which to feed them. Having prayed, the holy virgin milked the cow and drew forth enough milk to quench the thirst of that number of people.

On another occasion Samthann fed the abbot of Damlinis and one hundred and forty others with a small amount of flour, which she divided into two for a week.

The Death of Her Friend, Flann, and His Deliverance

There was a certain nobleman named Flann, son of Conla, who spent much time studying with the holy servant of Christ, Samthann. Whenever he was about to go to war, he would come to her for a blessing or a prayer. One time the men of Connacht attacked the men of Techua. Flann fought them, but he had not sought Samthann's blessing beforehand and he was killed. At the very hour when he died Samthann told her sisters of his death and spoke these words, "Give yourselves immediately to prayer, for now the soul of our friend Flann is being led by demons to painful places." After saying this, she fell into an ecstasy. Waking up a little later, she said to the nuns, "Render thanks to God because the soul for whom you have prayed has been taken from torment to peace through our prayers and God's immense compassion."

Samthann's Crozier

Niall, the son of Fergal, king of Ireland, asked for the crozier of the holy virgin that he might adorn it with gold and silver. But since the wood was crooked and old, the craftsmen thought it unfitting to ornament it. The following night the crozier was placed against the wall over the king's bed. Due to the devotion of the pious king and the merits of his servant Samthann, Christ straightened the wood so that no trace of crookedness was seen in it. The king rejoiced greatly because divine compassion had done what human power could not do. After that the king himself and his whole people held that crozier in the highest esteem.

On another occasion, as holy Samthann was returning from the monastery named Granard to her own, she came upon an oak tree of immense proportions. One of its branches grew across the road so that people seated in a chariot could not pass. The holy virgin placed her crozier against the obstacle, and laying it across the branches, ordered them to recede. The branch causing difficulties wound round the tree immediately, raised itself on high, and provided them with an easy passage.

Samthann's Wisdom-Saying On Prayer

A certain monk once questioned Samthann about the way of praying. He wondered whether a person should pray lying down, sitting, or standing. She replied: "In every position, a person should pray."

Samthann as Maelruain's Confessor

A certain itinerant peddlar in Munster in the time of Samthann used to carry greetings from her to the Celi De (sons of life) in that country. Once she called him to her and made him agree not to add to or take away a single word from the following messages. Then she said to him: "Tell Maelruain for me that he is my favorite among the clerics of the desert. Another thing, ask him whether he accepts women for confession, and will he accept my soul friendship?"

The peddlar took her message. But when he told Maelruain that he was Samthann's favorite, the monk rose at once and raised both hands as in a cross and gave thanks to God. When the peddlar asked him next whether women sought spiritual advice from him and whether he would accept Samthann's soul friendship, he blushed down to his breast and made three genuflections, then fell silent for a long time. Then he said: "Tell her that I will seek spiritual advice from her." Then the peddlar told all those sayings to Samthann, and she said: "I think, something will come of that youth."

On Study, Pilgrimage, and Prayer

A certain teacher named Dairchellach once came to Samthann and said: "I propose to give up study and give myself to prayer." She replied, "What then can steady your mind and prevent it from wandering, if you neglect spiritual study?" The teacher continued, "I wish to go abroad on pilgrimage." She replied: "If God cannot be found on this side of the sea, by all means let us journey overseas. But since God is near to all those who call on him, we have no need to cross the sea. The kingdom of heaven can be reached from every land."

Her Outstanding Qualities and Death

These are but a few of Samthann's many wise sayings. For who could relate all the things with which God enriched her? She was filled with the grace of good works, adorned with the beauty of all virtues, enriched by the good deeds of her whole life—this holy mistress of those under her, but the humblest servant to them all. She was poor in spirit and in possessions. She refused to possess lands and never had more than six cows. She was extremely careful in her charity to everyone but especially to those of her own household. To give but one instance of this, she divided the alms offered to her among the sisters. She so identified herself with every cell of her community that no matter what number of sisters were living together in each one, Samthann divided her share with all. She was joyful in giving, shy in accepting, gentle in compassion, mighty in helping. She never omitted an act of devotion. And so in holiness and justice before her spouse, Christ, she completed the course of her present life on December 19 and received the crown God has prepared from eternity for those who love him.

On the night on which she gave her soul to heaven, the holy abbot Laserian saw with his eyes wide open two moons, one of which came down to him. Remembering his request to her that she bend toward him when she was going to the heavenly kingdom, he recognized that she was in the form of a star. He said, "Well done, faithful servant of God, Samthann, because you are now about to enter the joy of your Lord and Spouse." Thus she disappeared, ascending to heaven where she enjoys eternal life for endless ages.

Conclusion

God is glorious in his saints.
The Voyage of St. Brendan

There is a painting in Florence, Italy, by the medieval artist Fra Angelico entitled, "Entry of the Blessed into Paradise." Filled with vibrant deep reds, blues, greens, and golds, the scene depicted is that of saints and their angelic companions engaged in a joyful circle dance. Holding each other by the hand, they move together toward the radiant gates of the heavenly Jerusalem from which golden beams of light emanate. The linkage of their hands symbolizes the common journey they are on and the friendship they share.

An aspect of the painting that may be overlooked initially is the direction of the rays of light and what they shine upon. Passing through two angels and illuminating a path in which the circle dance can move, they fall directly upon a beautiful tree, filled with ripened fruit. This tree appears similar to the tree Ciaran and Enda saw in their vision so many centuries ago, growing in the middle of Ireland and sheltering birds of the air.

For me, this splendid work of art with its powerful symbols of light, circle dance, and sacred tree represents the wisdom of the saints, all those holy people through the ages who have been—and are!—passionate in their pursuit of wisdom and the holy life. Abba John, one of the desert Christians whom the people of the early Celtic church so admired, compares the saints themselves to a group of trees, "each bearing different fruit, but watered from the same source." Poets have celebrated this holiness and wisdom, equating it with great felicity, and acknowledging, as Dante does, that "where this Love [of Wisdom] shines, all other loves grow dim and almost spent."

This book has been about the wisdom of the Celtic saints, a wisdom of the mind and heart originating in their spirituality and expressed in their soul friendships. Many of us today long for such wisdom. We yearn for trustworthy guides who can point us in the direction of genuine happiness and true fulfillment. We hunger, at the deepest core of our being, for communion with others and intimacy with God. The great spiritual traditions recognize this

---

201

human need, and they, as well as modern artists, playwrights, writers, and psychologists, speak of the value of consulting ancestors in our search.

Black Elk, the Native American shaman mentioned earlier, tells of praying to his grandfather in words reminiscent of Ciaran's and Enda's vision: "Hear me, you who have the power to make grow! Guide the people that they may be as blossoms on your holy tree. Make it flourish deep in Mother Earth and make it full of leaves and singing birds." Another holy man, St. Seraphim, a nineteenth-century Russian *staretz* (spiritual guide), asked his followers to visit him after his death: "Whatever is on your soul, whatever may have happened to you, come to me as when I was alive, and kneeling on the ground, cast all your bitterness upon my grave. As you spoke to me when I was alive, do so now, for I am living, and I shall be forever." Black playwright August Wilson referred once in an interview to "blood memory" and how it can help us in our work: "Just open yourself to it; when your back is pressed to the wall, go to the deepest part of yourself, and there will be a response: it's your ancestors talking."

May Sarton alludes in her journals to "a kind of ocean depths of memories" where "time past" and "time present" flow together and the dead live on. So too Carl Jung speaks of "ancestral components" that dwell within each of us and which we must come to know if we are to escape what he calls "loss of soul." All are in agreement that our ancestors can act as spiritual mentors, teaching us about living gracefully and dying with less fear.

Christian Celts considered the saints, especially those native to Ireland and Britain, their oldest ancestors. They believed that the saints were not only tribal protectors but family members who cared for them from beyond the grave. These saints were held up for imitation, not just as dead heroes who could inspire, but as living soul friends to whom they could pray and from whom they could receive ongoing guidance and support. Theirs was a relationship of mutuality in which they sometimes prayed *for* their departed relatives and at other times *to* them "as if," the Rule of Columcille says, "every faithful dead were a particular friend." This deep respect for the dead and love of their ancestors was reflected in their "baptizing" the ancient pagan Celtic feast of Samhain on November 1 into the great Christian celebration of the Feast of All Saints. It is expressed visually in the high crosses, with their wonderful images and stories in stone. It is revealed in the hagiographies of the saints, written so long ago in the monasteries of the early Celtic church, which can still teach us about ultimate realties.

If we look closely at the stories and sayings of the saints found in this book, we find that in their own way they constitute what Ita recommended that Brendan learn: "the rule" of the Celtic saints. This rule cannot be defined precisely for everyone, for it presupposes that Christians who follow it have, like the saints themselves, a great variety of personalities, experiences, and gifts. It does not consist of a multitude of minute laws or exhausting regulations, although it would certainly encourage the development of such daily disciplines as those found among the early Celtic Christians: proper diet, physical exercise, work, study, and prayer, as well as time and leisure with one's family and friends. It is definitely not about a new standard of perfectionism, which produces only increased anxiety, guilt, or shame. Rather, what this rule consists of is one of the simplest and hardest lessons of all: compassion, a profound respect for and love of all creation, beginning with ourselves.

A person does not acquire this wisdom instantaneously as if it is some new possession purchased off a shelf; one cannot gain it in total isolation, for it involves, as Jesus taught us, relationships with self, others, and God. It is a rule rooted in our spirituality and in our friendships, and we must be patient with each other as we seek to live by it. We need to let this rule grow gradually in us, as Kevin patiently let the blackbird build her nest in his outstretched hand.

This rule of the Celtic saints can be learned firsthand by placing ourselves in the presence of our spiritual ancestors and allowing them to teach us by the example of their lives. By listening to their stories, we can begin to identify and accept our own strengths and limitations, both as God's gifts to us and as our gifts to our families, friends, and communities. By being attentive to the stories of the saints, we can also start to acknowledge and develop further those qualities we already possess and that the saints' lives manifest:

- Aidan's grace of discretion and love of the poor;
- Brendan's collaborative nature and bravery in facing the unknown;
- Brigit's extraordinary compassion and willingness to serve those whom no one else would touch;

- Canair's prayerfulness and courage in challenging even a saintly old man about the exclusion of women from full participation in church life;

- Ciaran's great capacity for friendship and desire to share what he had;

- Columcille's love of study and hospitality toward all creation, even an exhausted crane;

- Cuthbert's passion for solitude and a tearful gentleness that allowed others to open their hearts to him;

- David's and his monks' awareness that nothing can be called "mine" or "thine";

- Ethne's and Fedelm's persistence in asking questions about God and the ultimate meaning of their lives;

- Findbarr's ability to heal sicknesses of body and soul, surely because he was aware and accepting of his own;

- Hild's perceptiveness in seeing and helping Caedmon name and claim his talents, the foundation of his creativity and ministry;

- Ia's placing her life in God's hands and letting go of the results;

- Ita's thirst for holiness and dedication to listening to her dreams;

- Kevin's appreciation of nature's beauty and willingness to leave his solitary place for the sake of others;

- Maedoc's sensitivity to suffering and his giving himself permission to grieve at the loss of a friend;

- Monesan's incessant longing for God, which took her to foreign shores;

- Non's willingness to forgive and get on with her life;

- Patrick's openness to letting the spiritual realm, including angels, lead him;

- Samthann's knocking frequently on "the doors of mercy."

Perhaps this quality of Samthann's is the most important lesson any of us can learn from the Celtic saints: how significant prayer is and how much it can change us and the quality of our lives. As all the saints' stories reveal, miracles of transformation, healing, and forgiveness happened precisely when each of them turned to God in prayer. It is in prayer that we begin to discern the right direction to take when we are perplexed. It is through prayer that we receive the courage to accomplish what God, neighbor, and our deepest selves are calling us to do. It is when we pray that we are able to surrender to a higher power one day at a time, accepting whatever comes. It is the practice of prayer that can teach us true wisdom, the wisdom of compassion, the wisdom of the heart.

With this compassion we come to realize that we cannot expect ourselves to have *all* the qualities of the saints. After all, none of them was perfect either, and each had his or her own demons that resulted in sleepless nights and stressful days. No, the only expectation that should be ours is that, like the saints and Jesus himself, we are willing to use what we do have—not for our own self-aggrandizement, but for the glory of God and the service of God's people. As the saints discovered long ago, marvelous things happen when we let go of our own need to control and begin to live a little more with the wonder and trust associated with a child.

To read the stories and sayings of the saints and to listen to them with the heart is to rediscover the wisdom the early church already knew: being a saint is the vocation to which we all are called, not just the "greats" who lived long ago or those whom the church now officially canonizes or beatifies. Being a saint is simply centering our lives in God's and, through our ministries, helping others discover that God's compassion and forgiveness embrace everyone.

To reflect prayerfully on the lives of these early Celtic saints reveals that wisdom is nothing more—and nothing less—than knowledge of self, compassion for others, and friendship with God. If we cultivate those qualities and relationships in our lives, Christ and the saints will truly live in us, as we live in them.

The wisdom of those saints is still very much alive. Like the tiny coracle boats of the Celtic missionaries skimming swiftly over the ocean depths, they travel on in our dreams and our imagination. They give us a rich vision of a more inclusive church, and perhaps new directions in our own spirituality. They teach us the importance of friendship, and how it is a vehicle to God. They challenge us to be attentive to and more trusting of the gentle yet ever persistent call of God in our human experiences and in our hearts.

Bibliography of Primary Sources
and Recommended Readings

Allchin, A. M., and Esther De Waal. *Threshold of Light: Prayers and Praises from the Celtic Tradition.* Templegate, 1988.

Bieler, Ludwig. *Ireland: Harbinger of the Middle Ages.* London: Oxford University Press, 1963.

_____. *The Patrician Texts in the Book of Armagh.* Dublin: Dublin Institute for Advanced Studies, 1979.

Bitel, Lisa. *Isle of the Saints.* Ithaca: Cornell University Press, 1990.

Bowen, E. G. *The St. David of History.* Aberystwyth: University College of Wales, 1981.

Chadwick, Nora. *The Age of the Saints in the Early Celtic Church.* London: Oxford University Press, 1961.

Colgrave, B., and Mynors, R.A.B., eds. *Bede's Ecclesiastical History of the English People.* Oxford: Oxford University Press, 1969.

Condren, Mary. *The Serpent and the Goddess.* New York: Harper & Row, 1989.

De Paor, Maire and Liam. *Early Christian Ireland.* London: Thames and Hudson, 1978.

Doble, Gilbert H. *The Saints of Cornwall.* Oxford: Holywell Press, 1970.

Duckett, Eleanor. *The Wandering Saints.* London: Catholic Book Club, 1960.

Farmer, D. H., ed. *The Age of Bede.* New York: Penguin Books, 1965.

Flower, Robin. *The Irish Tradition.* Oxford: Oxford University Press, 1948.

Gougaud, L. *Christianity in Celtic Lands.* London, 1932.

Green, Miranda. *Symbol and Image in Celtic Religious Art.* New York: Routledge, 1989.

Hanson, R. P. C. *The Life and Writings of the Historical Saint Patrick.* New York: Seabury Press, 1983.

Hughes, Kathleen, and Ann Hamlin. *Celtic Monasticism.* New York: Seabury Press, 1981.

James, J. W., trans. *Rhigyfarch's Life of St. David.* Cardiff: University of Wales Press, 1967.

Kenney, James F. *The Sources for the Early History of Ireland: Ecclesiastical.* Dublin: Irish University Press, 1929.

Mackey, James, ed. *An Introduction to Celtic Christianity.* Edinburgh: T. T. Clark, 1989.

Matthews, Caitlin. *The Elements of the Celtic Tradition*. Worcester, England: Element Books, 1989.

McNally, Robert, ed. *Old Ireland*. New York: Fordham University Press, 1965.

McNeill, John T. *The Celtic Churches*. Chicago: University of Chicago Press, 1974.

O'Donoghue, Noel D. *Aristocracy of Soul: Patrick of Ireland*. Wilmington, Del.: Michael Glazier, 1987.

O'Dwyer, Peter. *Celi De: Spiritual Reform in Ireland, 750-900*. Dublin: Editions Tailliura, 1981.

O Hogain, Daithi. *Myth, Legend and Romance: An Encyclopedia of the Irish Folk Tradition*. New York: Prentice Hall Press, 1991.

O'Meara, John, trans. *Gerald of Wales: The History and Topography of Ireland*. New York: Penguin Books, 1985.

Plummer, Charles, ed. *Lives of Irish Saints*. London: Oxford University Press, 1922.

_____. *Vitae Sanctorum Hiberniae*. Oxford, 1910.

Reeves, William. *Adamnan's Life of Saint Columba*. Scotland: Edmonston and Douglas, 1874.

Richter, Michael. *Medieval Ireland*. New York: St. Martin's Press, 1988.

Roy, Charles. *Islands of Storm*. Chester Springs, Pa.: Dufour Editions, 1991.

Ryan, John. *Irish Monasticism*. Dublin: Irish Academic Press, 1931.

Sharpe, Richard. *Medieval Irish Saints' Lives*. Oxford: Clarendon Press, 1991.

Squire, Charles. *Celtic Myth and Legend*. Van Nuys, Cal.: Newcastle, 1975.

Stevens, J. *Bede's Ecclesiastical History of the English Nation*. London, 1910.

Stokes, Whitley, trans. *Lives of Saints from the Book of Lismore*. Oxford: Oxford at the Clarendon Press, 1890.

_____. *The Martyrology of Oengus the Culdee*. London, 1905.

Toulson, Shirley. *The Celtic Alternative*. London: Century, 1987.